Sober On A Drunk Planet: Quit Lit Series 2-In-1 Bundle

An Uncommon Alcohol Self-Help Guide
To Quit Drinking And Stay Sober.
For Sober Curious Through To Alcohol
Addiction Recovery.

By Sean Alexander

Table of Contents

Sober On A Drunk Planet:

Giving Up Alcohol

Sober On A Drunk Planet:

3 Sober Steps

Sober On A Drunk Planet:

Giving Up Alcohol

- The Unexpected Shortcut
To Finding Happiness, Health
and Financial Freedom

By Sean Alexander

To Mum and Dad
- through all the vomit, late-night taxi services,
drug dealer debt and drunken chaos that I caused,
you have always loved and supported me.
This book was only possible because you kept me alive
and out of prison!

A FREE GIFT TO YOU

Get your FREE E-Book on '7 Sober Secrets You Can't Ignore' by clicking the link below:

WWW.SOBERONADRUNKPLANET.COM

Introduction

Imagine teaching children that one of the most exciting things about becoming an adult is being able to take drugs.

Imagine convincing them that it's normal for good nights out to result in shaky, anxious mornings, with crashing headaches, empty wallets, and perhaps even vomit in the bed.

Imagine explaining that to have a "grown-up" holiday, adults may end up sleeping with people they don't like, get into fights, or wake up in a cell. They might not even remember any of it.

Don't worry kids, they're just normal "side effects".

It sounds mental. Because it IS mental.

We're not talking about illegal drugs (yet). We're just talking about socially acceptable alcohol. It's the drug children see everyone from their parents to their favourite celebrities partaking in. It's the focal point of funerals, birthdays, Christmas, holidays, weddings, christenings, divorces, bad breakups, dating, good weeks at work, bad weeks at work, getting a new job, leaving an old job, a drink before the game, after the game and probably during the game. The list goes on and on.

We live on a drunk planet.

Alcohol is everywhere and has been for centuries. Society teaches us that champagne means celebration, that a holiday is an acceptable time for drinking lethal cocktails in gigantic fish bowls, and that a dash of whiskey will help your child sleep. We're even taught that "hair of the dog" is the remedy for a hangover. And just when you think you've heard them all, someone rocks up claiming that a glass of wine is part of their "five a day".

As I said - MENTAL.

If alcohol were the magical, one-size-fits-all substance we're brainwashed into believing it is, why are there Alcoholic Anonymous groups in almost every town? Why do celebrities that consume too much of it instantly go from being respected to being shamed? And why do nearly 30% of young people now decide not to drink at all? (The Guardian, 2018).

There are plenty of answers to those questions.

In many cases, people are discovering - as I did - that quitting booze can set your life on an entirely different path.

People are deciding to get ahead in life and become sober on a drunk planet. They are fed up with the crippling hangovers, the shame, the hangxiety and the many other side effects of alcohol. They want to experience life sober with everything that it has to offer.

It's a path that's exciting, fulfilling and healthy - and it's also increasingly fashionable. Dealing correctly with your emotions, waking up hangover free and enjoying life to its full potential never gets old.

Most importantly, it could also be the one thing that finally allows you to look in the mirror and like what you see.

***

So, what brings you here?

Perhaps, like "the old me", you have a life packed with all the outward signs of success but feel empty inside.

Maybe you're beginning to tire of the whole "work hard, play hard" thing and struggling to see the point.

Are you living for the weekend and then spending half the week recovering from the weekend? You might not realise it, but you could be spending over 100 days of each year feeling the depressing and physically undesirable "side-effects" of alcohol. Imagine what you could do with your life if you were supercharged for all of those days?

There's little point in trying to come up with the precise definition of "a problem". People have many different reasons for wanting to reset their relationship with alcohol. If that weren't the case, there wouldn't be millions participating in initiatives like Dry January and Sober October every year.

Even Alcoholics Anonymous is becoming less anonymous. The world is starting to sober up, and celebrities talk more openly about their battles with alcohol and other mind-altering substances.

Perhaps you're beginning to wonder if that nightly wine to "take the edge off" is really a great idea. Or maybe you desperately need to stop waking up on Monday mornings with a frazzled brain and a wallet empty of everything besides screwed up cocaine wraps.

Those may sound like two opposite extremes, but they can be closer together than many expect. You may be thinking, "oh, I don't get bad hangovers", or "drugs? I'd never do DRUGS!"

Well, as we've established, alcohol IS a drug. And it's the one that many high-profile scientists classify as more harmful than any other (The Economist, 2019). For many, it's also a huge gateway - both to other drugs and to years of bad decisions.

Plenty of people spend years or even decades "getting away with it". Or at least they think they are. They don't notice how the hangovers start to eat into the week, the gradual weight gain, or the friends and colleagues creeping ahead in life.

For other people, unexpected events and life changes quickly see "sustainable" drinking morph into "I need to do something about this". Anything from increased work stress to a redundancy, relationship breakdown or bereavement can cause things to escalate.

Regardless of where you're at, you don't have to reach the fabled "rock bottom" to enjoy all the benefits of sobriety. In fact, many people who've moved on from drinking rave about similar benefits and positive life changes - whether they were full-blown addicts, fans of "wine o'clock", or binge-drinking "weekend warriors".

If you're in any way doubting your relationship with alcohol, that's all the evidence you need. Presumably, you're not questioning your relationship with broccoli or fixating on whether you should cut back on reading or walking?

That's because we all know, deep down, that humans weren't intended to have a life where everything - positive and negative - is marked with alcohol. Children manage to play and have endless fun without it. But then something shifts, and millions of adults become convinced nothing can be fun without a beer, a glass of wine or a G&T.

There's a better way.

***

As you'll already know, this book is about giving up alcohol. However, it's important that we define what "giving up" means in this context.

"Giving up" is emotive language. It suggests we have to do without something desirable and that it's a loss.

Well, here's the good news, it's not like that at all.

If you're spending just a day or two a week hungover, you're "giving up" 50-100 days of your life, EVERY YEAR. And that doesn't account for time spent thinking about alcohol, planning occasions around it, and dealing with the chaos it can cause. Depending on how far down the rabbit hole you are, it could be consuming half of every year - or more.

THAT is a massive loss.

Similarly, you probably "gave up" many things as you reached adulthood: dreams, interests, and hobbies. If you followed the same trajectory as most people in the modern world, you probably swapped them for "going out". And for many people, "going out" means drinking.

I'm not for a moment saying that getting out there, partying and becoming an adult isn't a rite of passage and an awful lot of fun. But it IS part of the conditioning that makes alcohol such a crucial part of many people's lives. It's also where - for many - the bad habits begin to build.

Here's the fascinating part that's much-discussed in sobriety communities: It's not about what you give up; it's about what you get back.

One of the most used sayings within sober communities is that: "Sobriety delivers everything alcohol promised". You hear that one a lot because it's true.

The one thing that surprised me the most was how quickly sobriety delivers.

When you start to see how drastically different life is without alcohol, you begin to understand how much it impacted everything: health, relationships, finances, career and the spiritual side of life.

Think back to childhood and how "into" things you used to get before your time was taken up with the pressures of adulthood. Maybe it was sport, music, gaming, or one of a thousand other things.

That joy of being "at play" is still available to adults, but many swap it for the (empty and expensive) pleasure of heading to the bar for happy hour instead. The irony of "happy hour" is that yes, you might be happy for the hour or the evening, but if you are anything like I used to be, there's nothing AT ALL happy about the next few days!

The reality is that you do gain much more than you lose when you quit alcohol.

Not only do you get that child-like enthusiasm back, but you also get to enjoy all the same things you enjoyed before: holidays, nights out, dating, Christmas, birthdays, friendships, sex!

That little list shows, once again, how alcohol pops up everywhere. Over time, we come to associate it with all of those things. We wonder if we'll ever enjoy them the same way again. Well, along with millions of other sober people, I can assure you that you can.

And if you're thinking of how much you "love the taste" of specific drinks, there's a booming alcohol-free market catering to all the new non-drinkers. Long gone are the days when you only had one alcohol-free option on offer to you and were mocked by everyone in the pub for ordering it.

There are also much deeper issues to think about - and they're all things that giving up alcohol can improve.

If you're constantly worried you're not reaching your full potential - giving up alcohol can be the motivational rocket you need to get started.

If you need to repair damage to any area of your life - your health, relationships, finances, or career - giving up alcohol can be the missing key to turning your life around.

And if you search your soul and aren't all that convinced that you like yourself - giving up alcohol will allow you to heal.

Once again: you WILL gain FAR more than you lose.

***

So, what exactly will you gain from reading this book?

Here's a quick rundown:

First, you will discover the exceptional health and fitness benefits of quitting drinking.

Even a relatively small amount of alcohol can be incredibly damaging for your weight, skin, gut, and brain. Alcohol is a poison that the body isn't designed to process - hence why it comes in diluted form and why "alcohol poisoning" exists.

I can assure you that comments like "you look ten years younger" and "wow, you've lost weight and look amazing" never get old.

After health, we move on to finances. Drinking is expensive to start with, and it's also a substance that compromises your judgement and often leads to poor financial decisions.

Have you ever pressed the big red "f*ck it" button when you have had a few drinks, only to regret it financially for months or even years to come? It took me six years to fully pay off the debt from a last-minute holiday to Las Vegas! Four nights of "fun" for six years of debt. That doesn't seem like a fair trade!

I used to work in London's financial industry on a decent salary, but I STILL lived paycheck to paycheck. Quitting drinking can transform your finances - whether you need to get out of debt, buy your first property, or simply want to start saving and growing your money. And you can do all of this quicker than you might expect.

Next, we look at relationships, spanning everything from dating to parenthood. No more relying on a few glasses of wine to calm your nerves before a big date. Sober dating is as raw as it gets!

Relationships do change if you're living a sober life, especially if drinking was a large part of it before. Thankfully, I can assure you that they change for the better.

After that, we talk about personal growth. Drinking alcohol, even just a couple of times per week, can create a significant negative feedback loop. A night out leads to a hangover, which leads to junk food and laziness. You then begin the following week with low motivation (and a scary bank balance) and crawl your way through to "Thursday is the new Friday" before doing it all again.

NOT drinking creates a different feedback loop, but a positive (and much better) one. Imagine waking up on a Monday morning with more motivation and money than you expected, and that happening week after week. This is where changes happen *fast*.

It's little wonder that so many sober people report huge achievements in the months and years after quitting drinking.

After talking about personal growth, we get spiritual, and that doesn't mean talking about God, unless you want it to. As David Bowie once said, "religion is for people who fear hell, spirituality is for people who have been there".

Many people who quit drinking find that the empty feeling of living week to week is replaced by something very different - the complete feeling of a well-fed soul. This chapter also touches on the (entirely optional) 12 step programme.

Next comes the FUN of being sober. It's a different kind of fun, but it's far from boring. I can assure you that the millions of sober people don't just sit at home feeling bored! They're socialising, dating, achieving, and up early, indulging in hobbies while the drinkers sleep off Friday night.

We then talk about business and careers. While there are plenty of "functional" drinkers out there, an alcohol-free life enables you to take things to the next level.

A hangover-free life is, in itself, enough to transform a career. But add in the compound effect of constant clarity and extra energy, and things can get exciting at lightning pace.

In the final chapter, we look at the realities of being sober on a drunk planet. Booze is everywhere, and it doesn't disappear because you decide to stop partaking in it. The chapter looks at the environments you spend your time in and how they can change and evolve (for the better) when you stop drinking.

***

It's time for me to tell you a little more about myself.

I've been the once-per-week drinker, but I quickly became the finance job, flash car, nice house, high salary, drinking all weekend and ruining the week kind of drinker.

Full-blown drug addiction wasn't far behind.

I was never somebody who stopped at just one drink. The first time I went to the pub at the age of 14, when all you needed to get served was a friend who reached puberty early, I drank too much. My drinking has always been the same. It was never just one. Never.

The same thing happened with my drug-taking. I never had one line of cocaine - I had to have the whole bag.

University was a big catalyst that escalated my drinking. The drinking was heavy. I blacked out a lot, and alcohol-induced vomiting was often a feature. But it wasn't a problem, because - well - everyone else was doing it.

This pattern of drinking continued until I left university.

Then I found COCAINE - another substance that many movies would have you believe is the height of glamour.

Cocaine seemed to cure all the issues I had with alcohol. It stopped the booze-induced vomiting, which allowed me to drink more. I started to remember everything and feel like I was in total control.

The trouble was that I'd just swapped one drug's side effects with the equally debilitating impacts of another: My hangovers became "changovers" (cocaine-induced sleep deprivation). The cost of a night out quadrupled, and my underlying paranoia and low mood got increasingly worse.

Alcohol and drugs were "fun" for the first couple of hours of a night out. But then, my inability to stop meant I would always regret everything the following day. I'd have a horrible hangover. I'd beat myself up for making bad financial decisions. I'd hate myself for not going to the gym. I'd remember awful comments I'd made the night before. I'd eat poorly - again.

The same cycle of behaviour lasted for 17 years.

Albert Einstein once said that "insanity is doing the same thing over and over again and expecting different results". Every Sunday, I would tell myself that the next week would be the week I "got my sh*t together". But then I did what I always did - and got drunk.

By the time I reached my thirties, my hangovers had gone from lasting a few hours to lingering all week. By this point, a night of drinking and drug-taking was more akin to self-harm than being an "epic night out".

Attempts to "fix" myself and move to Thailand, Australia and South Africa didn't cure the problem I had with alcohol. They actually made it much worse.

Anonymous groups call this "doing a geographical".

Your problems don't magically disappear because you are in another place. Moving around can, in fact, isolate you even more - and give you more reasons to drink and drug.

Over time, it became very clear that external things weren't fixing my internal problems.

The "work hard, play hard" lifestyle turned into a "play hard all the time, and hope work doesn't fire me" lifestyle.

Luckily, I made it through without getting sacked. However, I'm sure plenty of ex-employers thought that I was sh*t at my job. That's because I was horrifically hungover or still drunk and high much of the time.

Having lost everything to addiction, I eventually reached my personal "rock bottom". With nothing to my name other than a private medical policy, I finally asked for professional help and checked into rehab.

Rehab saved my life. It gave me the time to stop living in the same cycle of behaviour. Most importantly, I finally began to learn why I was drinking and drugging.

It became clear from my time in rehab that I'd been unhappy with how I looked and felt. That started way back when I was a child. Alcohol was my "medicine". It would "take the edge off my insecurities". The more insecure I felt, the more I drank and drugged.

After rehab, a considerable amount of family support, personal development, and having done the 12-step programme by attending Alcoholics Anonymous, Cocaine Anonymous, and a few others, I'm a very different person. Only once I gave up alcohol did I realise how "allergic" I was to it and how negatively the "reactions" impacted every area of my life.

As soon as I left rehab, I got a personal trainer and shifted 35kgs (77lbs) in just four months, mainly down to getting sober. The effect of getting fit coupled with getting sober was incredibly transformative. I managed to hold onto my job and then saved the money I needed to jump ship from the corporate world and start my own business.

With all the time and energy that sobriety has given me, I have been able to re-train as a counsellor, produce a sober podcast series and become a strength & conditioning coach and yoga instructor. Helping people get stronger, both physically and mentally, is why I love my new career and I'm able to bounce out of bed at 6 am each day.

I feel like I finally have a purpose to my days. All thanks to getting sober.

I've gone from the brink of bankruptcy to having savings, a roof over my head and a heart full of gratitude.

Most importantly, getting sober has finally turned me into someone who can look in the mirror and be proud of what he sees.

I wrote this book to help you question your relationship with alcohol and hear that life without alcohol can be AMAZING. Giving up alcohol does present some challenges, especially if you have never known anything different, but you deserve to understand why nobody ever regrets getting sober.

The benefits that I share with you aren't just benefits that have changed my life but gifts echoed across the ever-growing sober community. It doesn't matter if you identify as an addict, are someone who suffers "hangxiety" from their weekly night out, or an individual wondering whether alcohol is really your "friend". The benefits are for EVERYONE.

So what are those benefits?

They include looking (and feeling) younger and fitter, having more money, and having almost constant energy and clarity. This feeds into incredible careers, deeper relationships, fulfilling weekends, rejuvenating holidays - and even unbelievable sex!

Giving up alcohol makes you more driven, focused, and resilient. And it dramatically improves both your physical and mental health.

These benefits come quicker than you might expect, especially if alcohol plays a significant part in your life. You could see a marked change in yourself in just weeks, and the "upgrades" keep on coming as you get more sober time under your belt.

Giving up alcohol is INCREDIBLY TRANSFORMATIVE for every area of your life, and I can't wait to help you experience it for yourself.

***

Are you ready to benefit from the life-changing advantages of giving up alcohol and becoming sober on a drunk planet?

Let's begin by learning how to like what we see in the mirror. That starts with health and fitness - and giving up alcohol is one of the critical cheat codes for that.

Chapter 1:

The Sober Glow

We've mentioned looking in the mirror a couple of times already. There's a good reason for that.

Your reflection in the mirror is one of the first things you see every morning, and you keep on seeing it all day.

I came to hate my reflection.

Over 17 years of binge drinking, eating takeaways, drugging and smoking cigarettes, it's no surprise I wasn't happy with my appearance. You are what you repeatedly do.

My weight skyrocketed after university. Over time, I put on 51kgs (112 lbs). My skin was terrible, and I never felt comfortable in my clothes. It doesn't matter how much you spend on designer labels if you're not content with the body inside them.

Not only did I feel grotesque on the outside, internally, I was suffering as well. I had Irritable Bowel Syndrome (IBS) brought on by alcohol, cocaine and cigarettes, yet I managed to kid myself they weren't impacting my health. My blood pressure was dangerously high, and my nose was constantly streaming.

I was a mess, both inside and out.

And we've not even covered the turmoil that was going on with my mental health - another byproduct of being constantly disappointed by what I saw in the mirror. But alcohol and drugs "helped" me forget about it, one day at a time.

You can't avoid that mirror, and you either like what you see, or you don't. If you don't, well, that's chipping away constantly at your happiness and self-esteem.

That's why we begin this section by talking about the health benefits of quitting drinking. They are countless, and you can start to enjoy them fast: clearer skin, transformative weight loss, more muscle tone, and a massive boost in energy and clarity. All these health benefits are what we call the "sober glow".

That's a whole load of upgrades. And the best thing of all is that you can start to notice them within the first 30 days.

If you've been drinking regularly, without taking a prolonged break, you may not know what looking and feeling truly healthy can feel like. And, yes, going out for a "big one" once or twice a week does count as regularly!

Are you ready to find out how much better life can be?

Body Transformation: The Sober Method

Many of us drink to boost our confidence, reduce our inhibitions, and feel comfortable in ourselves and around others.

They're certainly the main reasons I drank so regularly.

The key reason for my boozing was that I was unhappy in my own skin. There's a cruel irony because the drinking, drugging, and all the things I was doing as a result (such as eating junk and failing to exercise) were causing me to put on weight. As such, I was becoming even less happy in my own skin.

It's an incredibly vicious circle. But it's not unusual. Millions of people follow the same path - week after week and year after year.

We'll come on to how insanely calorific and unhealthy alcohol is in a moment. But first, I must emphasise that it's not just the drinking itself. For me, the hangovers were doing at least as much damage. And I was hungover most weekends from the age of 15 to 31.

The longest I ever went without drinking alcohol during that period was one stretch of seven days. And that was only because I was on antibiotics.

Nobody does anything particularly useful during a hangover. Yes, you might make it to work and do the things you absolutely have to do, but then you return home and reward yourself with a takeaway. People don't do things they don't absolutely have to do when they have a hangover. Eating well and exercising are usually the first things that get neglected.

As such, when you're regularly drinking, you end up stuck in a really damaging pattern. You don't have a chance of sticking to a healthy lifestyle.

I tried, half-heartedly, to get fitter and lose weight. I knew I wanted to, and I knew my weight gain was making me unhappy. But I sabotaged my plans at every turn.

Diets never worked for me because I'd never manage more than a week before a drinking session, and its aftermath got in the way.

The gym was equally unsuccessful. I never stuck to any sustained fitness routine because my boozing routines got in the way. The only time I saw the inside of a gym during a weekend was when I decided to do a spin class whilst still steaming from the night before. Almost vomiting onto the rider in front of me taught me that I couldn't mix nights out with exercise the next day.

***

Plenty of people will tell you, often with a smug sense of superiority, that the secret to weight loss is simply to "eat less and move more".

It's annoying - but the thing is, they're right.

To be a little more scientific about it, you must be in a *calorie deficit* in order to lose weight. That means that you need to be burning off more calories than you're taking in. (Standard daily calorie recommendations are 2500 kcals for men and 2000 kcals for women). (NHS UK).

Simply ensuring you have that deficit is, in theory, enough to shed some weight. But the movement part is crucial too. Exercise helps you burn more calories, which helps towards a weight loss goal.

It's important to point out that losing weight isn't the only option. It's not everybody's goal and may not be yours, especially if you've managed to stay slender throughout your drinking days (I wasn't so fortunate!).

Health isn't defined by weight loss. Some people are more focused on bulking up and building muscle. Bulking up is achieved with a *calorie surplus* when you take in more than your recommended daily calorie allowance alongside doing suitable exercise.

Bodybuilders, for example, go through phases of calorics surplus when they want to build muscle and then a calorie deficit when they want to lose fat. This is what they term "bulking" and "shredding" phases.

As you know, I'm a strength & conditioning coach now, but I want to assure you I'm not on a mission to turn you into a gym addict! The point I'm making is what you look like in the mirror DOES come down to calories in and movement out.

And that takes us back to booze.

Alcohol is packed with calories, and they're also EMPTY calories. This refers to the fact that alcohol provides little more than an energy source, with little nutrients we need to be strong and healthy.

Alcohol contains 7 calories (kcal) per gram, which is nearly as much as fat at 9 kcal per gram. Protein and carbohydrates come in at 4 kcal per gram.

Calories are *not* equal. A portion of broccoli at 200 kcal is not the same as a 200 kcal bottle of beer. People who regularly skip eating meals for booze will be missing out on essential nutrients that our body needs to thrive.

If the only way to get drunk was to sit at a bar eating endless spoonfuls of sugar, it seems probable that fewer people would do it! But calories-wise, millions of people are doing something similar. There can be up to five teaspoons of sugar in just ONE pint of cider - close to the maximum you're supposed to consume each day. (DrinkAware).

It's no wonder that people who drink regularly struggle to lose weight and tend to see their weight gradually rise. The science backs this up, with a study showing that young adults who drink regularly have a 41% higher chance of becoming overweight. They have a 35% chance of crossing the line to "obese". (Fazzino, Fleming, Sher, Sullivan and Befort, 2017).

It's easy not to notice it's happening, and the people closest to you often fail to see it too.

You know how it works: When you see a friend for the first time in a year, it's instantly apparent whether they're looking better or worse, fatter or thinner. But when you see somebody every day, you don't notice a pound here or an inch there. That applies to seeing yourself too.

It's time to scare you with some numbers:

We've already established that booze contains a lot of pointless, empty calories, but exactly how many often shocks people. Just one pint of 5% strength beer contains 239 kcals (the same as a full-size Mars bar), and there are 216 kcals in a 4.5% pint of cider.

A double gin and tonic, often seen as the more "low calorie" option, still contains 180 kcals.

And the thing is, we don't usually just have one, do we? Sitting and eating six Mars bars back-to-back would be seen as "excessive", but it's not unusual for people to consume the same calories in beer on a casual night out.

It's when you add the calories up that it starts to get truly mind-blowing. When you look at the following table, remember those daily calorie recommendations: 2500 for men, and 2000 for women. And remember, these calorie recommendations are based on a balanced diet (fats, proteins and carbohydrates), not a balanced diet of different alcoholic drinks!

	4 Drinks ("Casual Night")	8 Drinks ("Late Night")	12 Drinks ("Big Night")
Pint of 5% strength beer - 239kcal	956	1912	2868
Standard 175ml glass of 12% wine - 133kcal	532	1064	1596
Double gin and tonic – 180kcal	720	1440	2160
Pint of cider 4.5% - 216kcal	864	1728	2592

Sources: NHS UK, Drinkaware.

Looking at that table, you can see that it's possible to blow an entire day's worth of calories with just one "big night".

But we've barely begun. You've not even eaten yet.

It doesn't help that we often eat highly calorific food when we drink - both at the time AND afterwards.

That's no coincidence. Scientific studies show that drinking alcohol "favours overfeeding". (Tremblay & St-Pierre, 1996). Overeating during or after a session is almost a biological inevitability!

So let's add in a cheeky Big Mac meal from McDonald's. Not the large one, just the less-indulgent(!) medium size. That comes in at 1080 calories (McDonald's).

If you have a "late night" on the G&Ts, as per the table above, and finish off by inhaling that burger meal on the way home, you've already hit 2520 calories. That's more than the recommended daily number for men and over 500 more than the recommended number for women.

And that's before you've accounted for any other food that day - no breakfast, no lunch, no snacks.

We're only talking about a "late night", and not a "big night". And we've not yet thought about the next day.

When the hangover kicks in, we want "hangover food" - greasy, salty food packed with fats and carbohydrates - such as fried eggs, bacon, chips and takeaways. It's no wonder there's always a queue of Deliveroo and Uber Eats drivers at McDonald's on Saturday and Sunday mornings.

My favourite hangover "cure" was always a Full English Breakfast.

Unfortunately, they typically come in at around 1300 calories. It's also a bit of a tradition to follow them with another trip down the pub. The cycle begins once again.

And I'm still not done!

As we've established, people with hangovers rarely choose exercise as their preferred activity. That means they don't burn off the calories either. An hour's training session in a gym can burn off 500-800 calories. Collapsing in front of Netflix or getting a cab back to the pub.....doesn't.

All of these numbers are bad enough when it's a one-off. It's when you start to look at the compound effect of doing it repeatedly that things become truly shocking.

When I was going out three times a week and making the poor food choices discussed above, I was consuming around 10,000 extra calories each week. That's an astonishing 52,000 calories per year - the equivalent of 48 Big Mac meals. It would take me 75 HOURS of running to burn that off.

At a slow jogging pace, a marathon run takes around five hours. So I would have needed to run 15 marathons per year to compensate. And I HATE running!

Of course, it wasn't happening anyway. With the paralysing hangovers I experienced, the gym wasn't getting a look in. The result was grimly predictable: consistent unhealthy weight gain every year, high blood pressure, an incredibly unreliable digestive system, and shattered confidence and self-esteem.

And what did I do to compensate for that? Yes, I drank more and took more drugs. The cycle didn't stop until the drinking stopped.

So far, we've concentrated on calories and weight, but alcohol has yet another sting in its tail, ready to catch out those who do manage to get some exercise in between drinking sessions.

A peer-reviewed study showed that consuming excessive alcohol makes the muscles less able to benefit from exercise, "impair(ing) recovery and adaptation". (Parr, Carmera, Arete, Burke, Philips, Hawley, Coffey, 2014).

So, even if you do manage to force yourself to the gym or out for a run, alcohol still compromises how much good the exercise does. If you're looking to build muscle rather than lose weight, alcohol compromises your ability to do that, too.

Talk about adding insult to injury!

***

It's crazy how vicious that circle of alcohol, poor food choices and lack of exercise truly is. However, the exciting part is that quitting alcohol creates a whole new circle - one that's as healthy and rewarding as the old one is depressing and damaging. This new circle is achieved through the "Sober Method".

Getting sober creates the time and energy to begin a fitness journey and become more active generally.

Once again, this isn't about turning you into a fitness fanatic. Even if you're a less "committed" drinker than I was, swapping the weekly session and its aftermath for 72 hours of healthier choices makes an enormous difference to your wellbeing.

There are plenty of ways to replace the "high" of a night out, but essentially it just needs to be something that gets you moving. Exercise creates a healthy and natural high. If it didn't, there wouldn't be gyms in every town and runners on every street!

Exercise is a great way to ease stress and manage your emotions. Since becoming a strength & conditioning coach, I've never had a client "regret" a training session!

Movement is medicine, and there are hundreds of choices open to you: hiking in nature, cold water swimming (not for the faint-hearted!), team sports, dance classes, pilates or yoga. Try all of them - you'll have plenty of time to in sobriety.

Let's consider a circle that's virtuous instead of vicious. It's strikingly similar to the "drink - eat - put on weight - repeat" circle we've just looked at, but it transforms your health rather than destroys it.

First off: avoiding alcohol, in itself, means taking in far fewer calories.

Next, avoiding making bad food choices - when drunk and when hungover - means even fewer calories consumed. You also consume far more nutrients that allow your mind and body to thrive.

Not drinking means no hangovers, which means motivated, enthusiastic mornings and days where you have time available to exercise - and the drive to do it.

More exercise means more calories burned. Together with taking in far fewer calories, you can achieve the calorie deficit that results in weight loss a lot quicker than when you were boozing.

Alternatively, if you're looking to bulk up and add muscle (rather than fat), not drinking means that you truly benefit from your workouts.

Exercise gives you a natural high that boosts your mood and improves your mental health. That's science, not false promises from a strength &

conditioning coach! Exercise causes your body to release good stuff like serotonin, dopamine and norepinephrine. (Wasylenko).

Ironically, they're also the chemicals our brain hungers for when drinking and taking drugs. Unfortunately, substances don't work the way exercise does. Drugs and alcohol tend to deplete the brain of what you need to feel good, leaving you depressed, anxious and unmotivated.

Just as the negative circle of drinking just keeps on going, the healthy circle does too:

Your boosted mood makes you more inclined to do more exercise, and the weight loss (or muscle growth) begins to make that reflection in the mirror more appealing to you. (It also becomes more attractive to others, but we'll get on to sober sex and relationships in a later chapter!)

You're able to properly build muscle because you don't have alcohol messing with your myofibrillar protein synthesis (yes, that's a thing!). That means that your body's shape improves as well as its weight.

Finally, there's no underestimating the compound effect on your mental health (more on that in a moment).

Just as you begin to like that reflection a little more, other people often begin to notice too.

I can assure you that your first "you're looking in great shape", or "wow you're glowing", gives you a feeling you'll never get from a Long Island ice tea or a line of cocaine. That "sober glow" is a genuine thing - an effect where you begin to radiate positive energy and look fantastic to those around you.

The "Sober Method" to looking great is a feedback loop that keeps on going - a feeling of "levelling up" that becomes compelling in itself. And it can start as soon as the first alcohol-free week.

If you're one of the many people who has tried repeatedly to lose weight or get fit in the past, it may well be that quitting alcohol is the catalyst that makes a remarkable difference.

The good and bad circles work in similar ways but provide polar opposite effects. It's unsurprising that you don't tend to get the results you want if you try to keep a foot in both of them.

You also have nothing to lose by trying a different pattern for a while. You're not giving something up, as we've said. You're just trying something new. Giving up alcohol could be the answer.

When I finally gave up my own bad habits, I lost 35kg (77lbs) in just four months. It gave me the confidence I'd spent years looking for in alcohol and drugs.

It was a transformation so powerful that I decided to become a strength & conditioning coach, keen to help others and demonstrate how much exercise can transform lives.

It's surprisingly common to see people who've chosen sobriety move into this line of work - I call it the “Life Coach Effect”. All have had their own transformation by giving up alcohol, and they want to help others experience the same thing.

Even if you’re somebody who doesn’t find exercise particularly appealing, there are plenty of ways to embark on your own fitness journey. Regular walking can create a time for podcasts, music, audiobooks and entertainment. Combine that with healthy eating, and you’re already on a path to life-changing benefits.

Don’t be surprised, however, if you start to become enthusiastic about more energetic activities, perhaps those you thought were beyond you before. The whole “look good, feel good” thing can get hold of you just as much as alcohol can.

A quick warning before we move on: If you are somebody who uses alcohol as a comfort blanket (as I did), there is the potential to find a new one elsewhere. For many, it ends up being food - most specifically, sugary food.

Sweets and other sugary treats make your body release dopamine, the "feel-good" chemical. Alcohol does that too, hence why many people end up with that "cross-addiction". Furthermore, if you've been drinking regularly, your body is used to all the sugar that's hidden away in the booze. (Silver Maple Recovery).

If you're moving away from regular drinking and the kind of excess calorie intake laid out above, you probably have plenty of leeway for some treats. However, it is wise to educate yourself on the sugar content of those treats and not become a regular at the cake shop instead of your local bar! Moderation in all things!

In the following sections, we move away from the fundamentals of the weight and shape of the body, and onto other ways, booze messes with your system.

You'd think that after making you gain weight and stopping you from building muscle, alcohol would be done with you - but far from it. It likes to punish you for your indulgences in other ways too - starting with the skin.

Wow - You Look 10 Years Younger

There's perhaps no worse time to take a selfie than when you have a hangover: bags under the eyes, dry lips, and skin that somehow manages to be both greasy and dehydrated at the same time.

Drink for years on end, and it becomes likely you never see a photo of yourself that you're entirely happy with.

Towards the end of my drinking days, I looked (and felt) 20 years older than my birth certificate said I was. The alcohol alone was making me look drawn, tired and unwell, let alone the cigarettes and cocaine. When the FaceID unlock on your iPhone stops recognising you on "the morning after", or the person on your passport photo looks like an imposter, alarm bells start to ring!

Many people readily associate alcohol with being bad for the liver - we'll come to that shortly. Fewer people seem to know how badly drinking impacts the skin. When you see "before and after" photos of people who have quit drinking, one of the most striking things is how much more they sparkle and shine. It's that sober glow again!

You either look "healthy", or you don't, and the dehydrated skin of a regular drinker doesn't tend to look good.

Here's the science bit: Alcohol affects the skin in various different ways (WebMD, 2020). First off, it dehydrates you, leaving you looking bloated and "puffy". The bags under the eyes come from the poor sleep that's almost inevitable when you drink.

Of course, if like me, you put drugs in the mix too, you may not sleep at all. Instead, you stare at the wall for six hours, desperate to get ANY sleep before the work alarm goes off.

As if "bloated and puffy" weren't enough, alcohol can also make you look red and flushed, sometimes developing into full-blown rosacea. This can become a long-term problem, leaving a constant redness, as can rhinophyma, often known as “alcoholic’s nose”.

Some people have an allergy to alcohol that can result in hives, and booze can also trigger sun sensitivity. Then, in the long term, there are other conditions such as psoriasis, cellulitis and even skin cancer - all of which can be activated by alcohol.

Scary stuff, but scary stuff with a powerful solution: quitting alcohol.

Let’s go back to what you see in the mirror. Even if you're fortunate enough to avoid the more severe consequences, drinking alcohol will have a detrimental effect on your skin.

The fortunate flip side is that giving it up is almost certain to leave you looking younger, more radiant and fresh-faced. And who wouldn’t want that?

Having attended many Alcoholics Anonymous groups, I’ve spent plenty of time guessing the age of sober guest speakers. They always appear much younger than they are. The sober glow makes it very difficult to guess the age of anybody who hasn't been drinking for a while! Getting comments from people saying "wow - you look 10 years younger", when you walked around looking 20 years older than you actually were, never gets old either.

Next, we move inside the body, beginning with the gut. This may be an appropriate moment for a "Too Much Information (TMI)" warning.

The unavoidable truth is that alcohol makes some pretty grim stuff go on below the surface too.

Alcohol-Free Farts

The "garbage in, garbage out" cliche is stomach-turningly accurate when it comes to alcohol.

Ultimately, it's not a substance that humans were built to process. It IS poison, and the body rejects it as such. One place that this is brought into sharp focus is in the gut.

Being bloated and ending up with a beer belly (or wine belly) is the least of your worries here. Many drinkers, as I did, develop symptoms common with Irritable Bowel Syndrome (IBS). Bloating, gas, cramping, diarrhoea, constipation and stomach pain were all frequent symptoms that I thought were "normal" until I stopped drinking.

Not only did I suffer from IBS but the equally unsexy heartburn and acid reflux.

"Heartburn is a burning feeling in the chest caused by stomach acid travelling up towards the throat (acid reflux). If it keeps happening, it's called gastro-oesophageal reflux disease" (NHS).

The symptoms have been shown to be heavily triggered by alcohol (Pan, 2019) and I'm certain that coffee, smoking cigarettes and taking cocaine (which was my diet at the time) didn't help either. I would regularly wake up with heartburn and a sour taste in my mouth. This led to bad breath, more bloating (I really didn't need any help by this stage of my life) and it's hardly surprising that I was single for the majority of my drinking days!

The mad thing is, I accepted all these symptoms, as "normal" and constantly felt uneasy because I wasn't sure what my body would do next. You would think those symptoms alone are enough to put you off drinking for life, but there are plenty more to talk about.

Alcohol is linked to all kinds of other stomach conditions such as gastritis, ulcers, and the ominous-sounding leaky-gut syndrome. (Libbert, 2021).

The fact that alcohol dehydrates you is enough, in itself, to cause havoc on your digestion. Regular drinkers often tolerate bouncing back and forth between episodes of constipation (caused by dehydration and excess intestinal bacteria) and diarrhoea.

To make it all just a little worse, repeat spells of constipation can give you haemorrhoids. As if proof were needed that movies provide an unrealistic view of alcohol, we often see James Bond ordering a martini but are never shown him in the chemist asking for pile cream!

The simple fact is that your stomach doesn't want alcohol inside it. And the inconvenience of an "unreliable" digestive system can get a whole lot worse for those who cross the line into regular, chronic drinking.

Your overall level of health is hugely influenced by the health of your gut. (Recovery Nutrition, 2021). Poor gut health can put you in a position of systemic inflammation, which can increase your chance of Alzheimer's, heart problems, diabetes, Parkinson's, and various cancers.

There's plenty you can do to improve your gut health, hence store shelves lined with probiotic yoghurts, supplements, kefir and kimchi. But the one thing guaranteed to undermine everything else you do for your gut is pouring alcohol into it. Your digestive system doesn't want it - and will react accordingly.

Add in all the other things that come hand-in-hand with alcohol: bad food, poor exercise, and maybe drugs too, and it's no surprise your system kicks up a fuss.

No two bodies are the same, so your mileage will vary in terms of gut health. Perhaps you're not noticing any major effects - yet. However, it's extremely common for newly sober people to be taken aback by how much things change in that department.

For fear of painting too much of a picture, it's common for people's digestion to move from "unpredictable" to "regular as clockwork" after quitting drinking. Newly sober people often realise how much they'd come to "just put up with" things like indigestion, heartburn and a background feeling of nausea. It certainly was my "normal" when I was drinking.

The one thing that's indisputable is that quitting drinking will work magic for your gut health. And that involves far more than just food and digestion.

People often talk about "gut instinct" and "trusting the gut". The more that scientists research it, the more we come to realise just how much of a part the gut plays in our overall feeling of wellness.

The gut is often referred to as "the second brain". It links to the brain and plays a vital part in our feelings and intuition (Mind and Body Works). Expressions like feeling "sick to the stomach", or "having butterflies", emphasise this connection. Good gut health is key to good health more generally, both mental and physical.

After finally eliminating the chaos that alcohol wreaks on the digestive system, you are newly free to "trust your gut" - in more ways than one! Not only can you live a life without a mental map of the nearest toilet facilities, but you can also begin to support that "second brain" role that the gut plays.

As you build up sober time, you begin to get more in touch with your body, and with your "gut instinct". A dependable digestive system is, for many, a huge upgrade in itself, but the benefits can go way beyond just having alcohol-free farts.

That's enough "toilet talk" for now. Even though we've already mentioned some pretty terrifying illnesses, there's worse to come.

Shaking, Sweating And Hallucinating (Signs of Alcoholism)

So far, we've stuck to a light-hearted tone, despite references to several serious and life-threatening conditions that can be caused and exacerbated by alcohol.

There are no quips or funny analogies in this section: alcohol dependence is a deadly serious thing. Over three million people are killed by the "harmful use of alcohol" each year (World Health Organization, 2018).

Some people shake, sweat and have hallucinations when they go without alcohol. All of those are physical - and extremely dangerous - signs of alcohol dependence.

Others are as follows:

- Sweating.
- Hand tremors (shakes).
- Insomnia.
- Irritability.
- Anxiety and depression.
- Appetite loss.
- Headaches.
- Vomiting.
- Nausea.
- Fast pulse (above 100 beats per minute).
- Restlessness.
- Irritability.
- Disorientation.
- Breathing problems.

Source: Drinkaware.

Other issues can cause several of these symptoms, but the crucial point is that anybody who drinks regularly should seek professional medical advice before stopping abruptly.

Abruptly stopping alcohol and experiencing alcohol withdrawal syndrome can lead to seizures and sudden death. It's no joke, so always speak to your doctor before going "cold turkey". Specific symptoms to look out for include hallucinations, repeated vomiting and severe shaking.

Looking back on the symptoms I inflicted on myself, I'm extremely thankful that I stopped drinking and drugging. Although I got off relatively lightly in terms of physical withdrawals, my drinking and drug-taking resulted in numerous trips to the doctor, late-night visits to the emergency room, and overnight hospital stays.

You'd think that would be enough to shock a person into taking action.

It wasn't.

What can come next?

Nothing good: Liver conditions such as cirrhosis and fatty liver, strokes, heart disease, and many cancers including throat, colon, rectum, breast and mouth (CDC). The answer to what comes next is - sadly - serious illness and death.

Unfortunately, giving up drinking doesn't buy you a free pass to eternal good health. But it does drastically reduce the chances of a lot of bad things happening, and of you dying prematurely.

The science supports the likelihood of that happening. People who drink more than 18 alcoholic drinks each week can expect to live for four or five years less than non-drinkers. (Therrien, 2018). Even more, "moderate" drinkers, consuming 10-15 drinks per week, generally die one or two years before their time.

There's a lot you can do, achieve and enjoy in those years. And it's not only about your life being cut short. The time actually spent drinking and recovering can add up to many more years, as we will look at a little later.

If you're keen to determine whether you are drinking too much, or developing a dependence, Drinkaware has an assessment tool that is included in the resources section of this book.

I would emphasise the importance of speaking to your doctor if in any doubt. Alcohol is a widely available drug that affects millions of people. It won't be the first time they've helped somebody with it.

There are some further resources at the back of this book that can give you further help and guidance.

Next, we move from physical health to mental health - something that could be in short supply if you drink regularly.

Becoming Less Mental

I've already painted a pretty bleak picture of my life on alcohol and drugs. But it gets worse.

I lost count of how many times I woke up on an unfamiliar sofa - with no wallet, no phone, no keys, and no idea of what had happened the night before. Add in the raging hangover, and you have the dreaded "hangxiety".

So many days were spent piecing together the events of the night before and frantically trying to repair the damage - all whilst feeling shaky and sick, with a banging headache and a sense of impending doom and descending depression. And then I had work on Monday!

It's little wonder that "you never regret waking up without a hangover" is such a sober cliche.

What makes those hangxiety days even worse is that you still have all the problems you had when you started drinking the night before. There's a good chance you've made them worse.

A “few beers” to get over some work stress? Well done, you still have the work stress, but now you have to do the presentation with shaking hands and an aroma of stale tequila.

“Some” wine because you were fretting about money? Congratulations, you now have even less money.

“Dutch courage” because you were worried about the big date? Well, you blew your chances when you started slurring, and they’ve already blocked your number because of the 2 am text messages.

Using alcohol to try to “deal with” feelings and emotions is laughably flawed. It’s incredible that anybody still tries to do it. Many ex-drinkers refer to it as “playing life on hard mode”.

Homer Simpson probably isn’t the first person you’d turn to for mental health advice, but there’s a lot of wisdom in the well-used quote: “To alcohol! The cause of, and solution to, all of life's problems”.

Alcohol doesn't fix mental health problems. It's not even a particularly effective crutch. Any relief it provides is short term, at best.

When you stop drinking, you begin to recognise the insanity of using alcohol to ease you through the awkward first 30 minutes of a social event. For some, the price of that is doing something foolish, and spending the next week regretting it. And, of course, you may regret certain things for years. I'm still ashamed of falling through the champagne tower at my friend's engagement party - sorry, Aimee and Matt.

However each night ends, you generally get an incredibly poor trade-off for 30 minutes of "taking the edge off".

Alcohol never helps with mental health problems. It adds to them. And, once again, science backs that up.

Alcohol is a strange substance. It initially acts as a stimulant, causing your brain to release dopamine, the "happy hormone" (Healthline). It increases your heart rate, boosts your energy levels, and lowers your inhibitions.

But alcohol is, first and foremost, a depressant. It also binds to your gamma-aminobutyric acid (GABA) receptors, which has a sedation effect. At its core, alcohol is a "downer" drug. It also inhibits glutamate, messing with your brain, nerve and memory function. (AddictionCenter).

Then, in another cruel twist of irony, it reduces your release of all that cheery dopamine (when consumed in larger doses). That, right there, is why so many people start the night upbeat but end it with a "sad head" or an "angry head".

The chemical tailspin continues after you stop drinking. While you're consuming alcohol, your body begins to release cortisol, known as "the stress hormone" (Buddy T, 2020). Your cortisol levels continue to "spike" for some time. Those who drink a lot need to wait for a WEEK until cortisol levels normalise (Loria, 2017).

Cortisol comes from the adrenal glands and is the thing that makes people edgy, jumpy and panicky. When the depressive, sedating effects of alcohol begin to wear off, the cortisol really goes to town. This often manifests itself when you wake up with a start at 4 am, heart thudding after a night of drinking, with a mouth drier than the Sahara desert.

The cortisol continues its assault in the days after a session, playing a large part in the “hangxiety”. Cortisol is widely known as “nature's built-in alarm system”. (WedMD, 2020). Is it any wonder that flooding your brain with it causes you to jump at your own shadow?

To add insult to injury, while cortisol is battering your mental health, it’s doing bad stuff to your physical health too. An excess of cortisol causes the body to release insulin, and the extra energy ends up stored as fat. (Hayes, 2018). It also joins in with the alcohol in making you crave junk food.

And it's not done with you yet. Excess cortisol makes it harder for the body to build muscle. And if you do exercise while it's flooding around you, your muscles will be more tense and susceptible to injury. It makes recovery harder too.

The really scary part is how long the cortisol effect can last. If levels of your key stress hormone can go haywire for a *whole week* after drinking, your mental health doesn't stand a chance. If you drink regularly - even weekly - the cycle of damage begins again before your brain has repaired itself from the previous assault.

There's no surprise alcohol is so often linked to depression and anxiety. It's an actual depressant, and it overloads your brain with a hormone that literally *causes* anxiety!

That makes quite a mockery of the whole "taking the edge off" theory, doesn't it?

Booze fogs up your brain, messes with your memory, and makes you far less able to deal with the inevitable challenges that life throws at you.

Thankfully, as with the physical side of things, you can repair the damage by quitting.

A study of recovered alcoholics showed "cognitive and mental abilities" returning to those who quit drinking, becoming "indistinguishable" from nonalcoholics of the same ages (DeNoon, 2006). There was a small exception around "spatial orientation". Recovering alcoholics may always be a little worse at reading maps and assembling flat-pack furniture!

Perhaps the most rewarding mental health "upgrade" from quitting alcohol is learning to cope with life's complications without chemical "assistance".

For example, newly sober people quickly realise that almost everybody is nervous at the start of a party or work event. It's not necessarily easy, but with time you realise that you relax and notice your inhibitions falling away after a short while anyway.

Just think about young children at a birthday party. They often cling to their parents at the start or stay at the edges of the room. By the end, they're tearing around the place and don't want to go home. That's not because they're drinking alcohol!

It all adds up to another one of those virtuous circles. Over time, you come to learn that you manage just fine without the crutch. That boosts your self-esteem, making you manage even better the next time. You also immediately remove the drunken misdemeanours and the hangovers.

There's a lot to be said for the "radical clarity" you gain when you stop drinking. You cease having to ask yourself whether you were too loud, too argumentative or too "over the top". You become able to own your choices and decisions, knowing it was you that made them, and not the booze.

And as with all of the positive effects of giving up alcohol, this compounds over time. Good decisions and positive experiences breed *more* good decisions and positive experiences - instead of bad breeding bad.

Giving up drinking isn't necessarily a magic cure for your mental health. There may well be anxiety, depression and other conditions remaining within the real, post-alcohol you. They could well have been why you started drinking too much to begin with. But at least you get a chance to know what you're dealing with.

Self-medicating your mental health with alcohol robs you of that chance. It's like trying to drive a car without an engine. You're not going to get very far.

When you're sober, and your mind, your body and your gut are able to operate as they were designed to, you become much more in tune with yourself. Your intuition sharpens, and you finally get to learn about your "baseline" moods and levels of anxiety. You begin to learn which situations you struggle with and to acknowledge areas where you might benefit from some help.

When drinking alcohol is the response every time you "feel a bit off", you never truly know how to manage thoughts, feelings and situations. You may be pleasantly surprised and find that you're considerably more "zen", purely due to quitting alcohol. However, you may also feel you need some extra assistance.

Getting some counselling/coaching can be a great way to build your self-awareness and work further on that intuition. We look at that in a little more detail later in the book.

Although there are no guarantees, many people do find that giving up alcohol vastly improves their mental health. Another sobriety cliche (there are lots of them!) is, "I always thought alcohol was relieving my anxiety - I didn't know it was causing it."

The only way to know for sure is to try sobriety out for yourself.

Doing Stupid Sh*t

The health implications of drinking too much are clear, but there are other dangers too. They can also have some terrifying impacts on your physical and mental health, and on your day-to-day life and your future.

The harsh truth is that alcohol can make you do some really stupid sh*t.

In the US, in one year alone, drunk drivers attempted 147 million car journeys (Masterson, 2022). Around one-third of deaths in car accidents involve a drunk driver.

Even though drink driving is illegal around the world (with differing limits on what is tolerated), attitudes in society towards drink driving are INSANE. The amount of times I have heard the saying ' I am a better driver when I have had a few drinks' shows how drunk this planet really is.

There are plenty of "nice people" serving long prison sentences for drink driving offences where they thought they could get away with it.

Deciding to get behind the wheel of a car after too many drinks is just one of the millions of acts of stupidity that can be triggered by alcohol. Even "superficial" trips and falls can leave you needing a trip to the hospital or with an injury you have to spend weeks recovering from and explaining away.

If you're a regular drinker, you may or may not have injured yourself whilst drunk. If not, you can probably think of a few times when you came close. Every time you overindulge, you're rolling the dice on that being the time when you wake up with more than just a headache and a sense of regret to deal with.

It's not just the risk of arrest, death and physical injury (although they should be bad enough). Lowered inhibitions and an impaired sense of judgement can seriously mess with your risk perception.

"Stranger danger" isn't just something children need to worry about. Drinking makes you vulnerable, and while you may "get away with" going home with random people many times, the next time could always be the time you put yourself in serious peril.

There is an inevitable sexual side to this, too: waking up next to somebody you don't remember meeting doesn't just fill you with shame, it also puts you at risk of STIs and unplanned pregnancies.

I could write a whole other book about the bad decisions I've made (and the terrifying risks I've taken) while under the influence. But I am fortunate; I ended up in rehab and not the other two places addicts go; prison or the local cemetery.

Alcohol was a gateway drug for me, as it is for many people. I didn't tend to buy cocaine when sober, but it became almost inevitable after the third drink. The risks around drunkenly buying drugs are many - from getting caught picking them up and being arrested, to inadvertently snorting rat poison. Once again, this is an area where you can "get away with it" a thousand times before coming unstuck the next.

All of these risks fit into this chapter on health because the knock-on effects can affect your health. Drunken escapades can fill you with shame, dread and anxiety even if the worst doesn't happen - and that's kryptonite for your mental health. You can spend weeks/months/years thinking about how close you came to disaster or wondering if your phone's going to ring (or the police will come knocking) about something you don't even remember doing.

And when your luck does run out, it can run out in spectacular ways. Any one of those 147 million drunken car journeys could end in arrest, prison time, a lost job or death. That's not melodrama or exaggeration - because many of them do.

It might never be you until it is you.

There's a reason - many reasons - why alcohol often tops the table in rankings of dangerous drugs. People often say that if it was discovered now, there's no way it would be legal. The fact it's a drug that's everywhere doesn't mean you're not playing with fire by using it. The next time could always be the time that things go seriously wrong.

***

The arguments for being sober on a drunk planet are already rather compelling: More confidence, better looks, no more pointless guilt, less chance of developing a serious illness that you will blame yourself for, and less chance of doing something you'll regret for the rest of your days.

But health and sanity is just the start. The next chapter talks about something most people want more of - money.

Chapter 2:

The Financial Freedom of Sobriety

Alcohol is expensive. Drugs are even more expensive. Late-night taxis are expensive. Takeaways are expensive.

It's all expensive. And it doesn't matter if you feel you "can afford it".

Working as a financial consultant in London, my salary was decent - well above average. But my inability to say "no" meant I kept going out and ending up with nothing left to show at the end of each month. I was choosing a lifestyle over everything. All I had was patchy memories, anxiety from drunken behaviour, and debt.

I managed to convince myself that I was living a life people dreamed of. And again, that cultural myth of the "glamour" around drinking and partying creeps in.

I now know how wrong I was.

The Cost Of Hangovers

In the previous chapter, we learned some hard lessons about the calorific cost of alcohol. Now let's look at the actual cost - Pounds and Pennies, Dollars and Cents.

For these examples, we look at some of the costs of a typical London night out. Different countries and cities vary, but it all adds up - wherever you are and whatever salary you are on.

It's all relative at the end of the day - if you spend more than you earn, you are in debt. If you save more than you spend, you are in credit.

We'll start with a pretty average "late night" on the G&Ts. The same one we discussed in the previous chapter - the one that weighs in at over 2500 calories.

Item	Cost Each	How Many?	Total
Gin and Tonic in a city bar.	£9 ($12)	8	£72 ($97)
Taxi home	£30 ($41)	1	£30 ($41)
Drunk food	£10 ($14)	1	£10 ($14)
Hangover food	£10 ($14)	1	£10 ($14)
		Total	**£122 ($166)**

US Dollar costs are based on an approximate exchange rate of £1/$1.36.

Perhaps £122 ($166) doesn't sound like that much. Or maybe it sounds like a lot. But remember, this can be calculated for whatever you earn and spend on a typical night out.

The above example represents a pretty tame night. If you do a "tame night" twice each week, those nights cost you £12,688 ($17,256) per year.

We've not even allowed for anything other than cheap takeaways, nor thought about the odd bottle of wine or pack of beer you purchase for a quiet night in.

Now let's look at the figures that made me too scared to check my bank balance for many years. Here's what a real all-nighter, aka the"big night" could look like for me:

Item	Cost per drink	How many?	Total
Pint of beer	£5 ($7)	6	£30 ($42)
Glass of wine	£7 ($10)	3	£21 ($30)
Cocktail	£12 ($16)	3	£36 ($48)
Round of shots	£30 ($41)	1	£30 ($41)
Club entry	£20 ($27)	1	£20 ($27)
Gram of Cocaine	£60 ($82)	2	£120 ($164)
Packet of Cigarettes	£12 ($16)	2	£24 ($32)

Taxi home	£30 ($41)	1	£30 ($41)
Food (Before and After)	£30 ($41)	1	£30 ($41)
		Total	£341 ($466)

US Dollar costs are based on an approximate exchange rate of £1/$1.36.

When you get truly caught up in the "party scene", the cost is staggering. The really crazy thing is that it almost becomes a badge of honour to have "a £341 night".

Everything in life is relative: You may not have nights quite like the one on the table above. I had MANY nights that cost MUCH more than that, especially those that started out with planned activities or began with a fancy meal.

That "£341 night" happened a lot.

Whichever way you do the sums, the end result is terrifying. Just one of those "big nights" every couple of weeks adds £8,866 ($12,058) to the annual "party lifestyle" total, bringing it up to £21,554 ($29,314).

And we've not even thought about what happens on holiday, at Christmas, on your birthday, on everyone else's birthday, at gigs and festivals, and at every other "special" occasion.

It's little wonder that despite my high salary, I always spent every penny. In fact, I went further than that and sunk into debt. I was living beyond my means and not even thinking about saving.

Debt's not unusual. 63% of adults in the UK have some personal debt (Calic, 2022). But I was in a good job with a good salary. I was also handing over more than £20,000 to bartenders, drug dealers and takeaway restaurants every year. There really was no excuse for being part of that statistic.

I would highly recommend calculating the rough annual cost of your own drinking. Don't just include the alcohol itself because - as we've seen - all of the associated costs add up too.

You may also need to include what I describe as alcohol-related "f**k it" moments - such as last-minute festival tickets and short trips to Las Vegas and Ibiza, funded by a credit card. These don't seem like shrewd investments when you look at them through sober eyes. Four days away can result in debt that can take literally years to pay off.

What makes these trips even worse value is that with booze and drugs involved, you usually get home needing another holiday to recover!

Even if your own total spent on "living it up" isn't as jaw-dropping as mine, it's still almost certainly a significant amount. Even a couple of half-decent bottles of wine each week adds up to over £1000 ($1351) each year - and that's if you buy them to drink at home.

Once again - alcohol is expensive.

And it gets worse.

Hangovers don't do your finances any good either.

People don't tend to think about investments, pensions and long-term plans when they have hangovers. It's enough effort to deal with the Deliveroo order and decide what to watch on Netflix.

So as well as spending too much and possibly borrowing too much, you're also doing nothing to move forward. It's possible to spend years doing this - as I did - whilst failing to notice that other people are getting ahead while you're standing still.

Do all this, week after week, and you're stuck in another one of those vicious circles we keep talking about.

Thankfully, it has the same powerful solution: giving up alcohol.

The Sober Bonus - £506,898 ($689,381)

Just as you can spend an incredible amount of money on going out drinking, you can save a significant amount by not doing it. The weight drops off, and the money begins to pile up!

This is another example of swapping a bad feedback loop for a good one.

In my case, alcohol was the gateway to all kinds of stupid stuff: gambling, buying drugs, eating fatty takeaways, and getting taxis instead of waiting three minutes for a train.

All of those were things I'd never do sober - so when I stopped drinking, they ALL stopped. That's a lot of money saved.

Newly-sober people are often shocked by how quickly they begin to save money. There are several reasons for this:

First off, sober people perform better at work. Let's shake off the whole "it doesn't affect my work" thing. It does if you're going through the motions and taking days off "ill" from work. People do notice when colleagues are grey and shaky in meetings, when they're late, when they smell of alcohol, and when they're the loudest and drunkest at work events.

As we covered in the previous chapter, quitting booze does magical things for your physical and mental health. Arrive at work with more energy, vigour and mental clarity, and people will notice. You will enjoy it more too.

That "sober glow" comes into play again. Your bosses will see the change in you - and all kinds of good things follow from that. More interesting work, more scope for promotion, bigger bonuses, and a real chance of getting a decent pay rise!

As a non-drinker, everything's different when 5 pm rolls around too. Suddenly, there are many more options beyond hustling to happy hour or heading home to nurse the previous night's hangover.

You quickly realise you have plenty of fuel left in the tank for side hustles, passion projects, second jobs and start-ups.

When you suddenly have a whole load of extra energy injected into your life, you feel like anything is possible - and it is. Many people in sobriety go on to become successful actors and actresses, publish books, become coaches, start businesses - and finally make money from the things they're passionate about.

Let's go briefly back to the "liking what you see in the mirror" thing.

Once you begin the process and start to build some self-esteem, you will become more comfortable with working on your own happiness.

It's easy to become conditioned to certain expectations: what work you can do, what you can expect to earn, what limitations you have. A lot of that conditioning begins at a very early age. But you can shake it off and begin to manifest better things for yourself. I highly recommend Dr Joe Dispenza's "Breaking the Habit of Being Yourself" for more on manifestation.

With alcohol out of the picture, you have more energy, more time, more confidence, more motivation, more money, more pride. You have less guilt, less debt, less shame - and less of a headache.

When you put all of those things together, you begin to see things very differently: Why NOT write the book? Why NOT move abroad? Why NOT start the business? Why NOT take up the sport you showed promise in as a kid? Why NOT try that career change?

The best part is that all those things you can do are probably things you *wished* you could do while you were still living for the weekend - the things you never got around to. Well, you can get around to them now.

Another side effect of this particular virtuous circle is that you can start thinking about the future. Saving and growing your money might not seem very "rock and roll" to the party animal in you - but reaching retirement age without a cent to your name isn't a good look either.

The first time you get to the end of the month with money leftover instead of an overdraft and a scary credit card bill, your mindset begins to change.

Maybe you could have investments, savings, and exciting long-term goals.

Drinking and drug-taking is a rather impatient way of obtaining short-term gratification - but it doesn't last. It's money that goes - quite literally - down the drain.

Delayed gratification, which comes with the power of saying "no", can allow you to reach goals you never thought possible before. And saying "no" doesn't mean being "boring". It means you're setting clear boundaries and not giving into the demands of others. Saying "no" doesn't mean giving things up, it means getting more in the long run.

Going back to the figures we looked at earlier, let's imagine you save the amount we arrived at for having a fairly tame night out a couple of nights per week (£12,688). If you managed to put that amount away somewhere where it earned 5% per year, you'd have around £190,000 ($258,400) in ten years. Nearly £50,000 ($68,000) of that would be interest.

If you went on a night out like I did, the numbers are even more staggering. If you do two of those big nights each week, you're spending £35,464 per year. Put that away for a decade at the same rate, and you have £506,898 ($689,381). Of that, £116,794 ($158,840) is interest.

(Source: The Calculator Site, Compound Interest Calculator).

Your own numbers will vary - but even if you're spending less, it still adds up to things like house deposits, weddings and new cars - perhaps all the above!

At this point, it seems right to emphasise something both cliched and unavoidably true: money cannot buy you happiness. As Will Rogers said, "too many people spend money they earned, to buy things they don't want, to impress people that they don't like."

Joking aside, you do learn in sobriety that buying "stuff" - faster cars, bigger houses, fancier holidays, and endless deliveries from Amazon - only delivers a similar, temporary happiness to drinking.

Excessive spending can even come with its own hangover, in the form of "buyer's remorse". This is the "feeling of regret" that often follows a large purchase, often triggered when you don't end up using the holiday home or the convertible as much as you expected, or when the purchase doesn't bring the happiness or feeling of satisfaction that you anticipated. It's highly likely you've experienced that feeling before!

We've said a lot about money in this chapter, but it's important to see it as a bonus, and not as the sole reason to give yourself a better life away from alcohol.

Inner wealth is always the winner, and that wealth comes when you're happy to sit with yourself on a Saturday night, not needing anyone or anything to make you feel content. Thankfully that comes as part of the sobriety package too, as we will come to in a later chapter.

Don't worry, you can be sober, happy AND rich! But health, inner peace and fulfilling relationships are more important for a happier existence. The relationships are what we move onto next - from friendships to the daunting practice of sober sex.

Chapter 3:

Sober Relationships

Relationships change when you stop drinking. Overwhelmingly, they change for the better - but it's important to know what to expect.

I can reassure you, right now, that sober people don't look back and wish they had their dysfunctional and toxic relationships back - so don't worry about what you might lose. You gain so much more.

In this chapter, we cover many aspects of how relationships change when you decide to be sober on a drunk planet - from dating to parenthood.

A theme that runs through all of this is that sobriety tends to give you much deeper relationships, but usually with fewer people. Nowhere is that more noticeable than with friendships - so that's where we'll begin.

The Sober Cull

Here's a scenario from my drinking days - one that played out literally hundreds of times:

I'd go into work on a Friday morning full of good intentions. This would be the weekend I'd get stuff done, play golf, eat well, sleep well, and not overspend.

But a colleague would suggest a "quick one" to shake off the stress of the week, or a mate would phone with the idea of a meet-up on the way home.

Ten drinks later, the weekend would be ruined, along with at least half of the following week.

This situation is familiar to millions of people and happens week after week, year after year: Weekend plans thrown out of the window and swapped for a brief feeling of being "fun" and "spontaneous", followed by days of feeling paralysed and paranoid on the sofa. What a waste.

People who drink regularly often find themselves in a crowd of "drinking friends". If you have a crew where every plan revolves around a bar or a club, that probably applies to you.

There's a famous quote from motivational speaker Jim Rohn, saying that "you're the average of the five people you spend the most time with." There's a lot of truth to that. If boozing is all your friends do, that's all you end up doing.

It's worth asking yourself what your friendships entail beyond the booze (or, if relevant, the drugs). Perhaps alcohol really is secondary, but it's not at all unusual for friendship groups to build up around nothing more than a shared passion for boozing.

If that feels familiar to you, don't worry. It may seem a little daunting to turn your back on that crowd, but I can assure you better things await.

If you are part of a group like that, you can expect two things to happen when you quit drinking - things that are often referred to as "the sober cull".

First, you may find some of the group shun you, or are dismissive of your efforts. Thankfully, in early sobriety, this can be a good thing. Initially, you won't be too enthusiastic about spending time with people who are drinking hard anyway.

The next thing that happens, as your confidence and self-esteem grow, is that you become more selective about who you want to spend time with. This quote from Rikki Gale is relevant here:

"I used to walk into a room full of people and wonder if they liked me... now I look around and wonder if I like them."

As you emerge as a newly-sober person, you'll almost certainly be keen to reevaluate who you want around you. Who do you want those "people you're the average of" to be?

Some of the sorting will be done for you: Be alert to the people saying "can't you just have one?" or "you're no fun anymore!" Those people may have to go. If they can't support your desire for a better life, they shouldn't be part of it. Perhaps your desire to confront your own bad habits is shining an uncomfortable light on their own.

As a sober person, you get used to saying "no". Once you've found the strength to say "no" to alcohol and drugs, saying "no" to a single night out is no challenge at all.

It's all about replacing the Fear Of Missing Out (FOMO) with the Joy Of Missing Out (JOMO). It's delayed gratification again, both on a short-term level and a long-term level.

By saying no to a Friday night in the bar, you get to spend the weekend doing the things you actually wanted to do. Longer-term, you have the money, energy and drive to work towards bigger and better goals.

There's genuine joy in settling down on a Friday night in fresh bed linen, knowing for certain that you'll be doing the activities you've planned for the weekend. Waking up early, fresh and inspired beats waking up in the wrong place without your money or your dignity.

True friends will be supportive of your desire to better yourself. Having those people contribute to your "average" is just fine. You may well uncover some surprises too. The stand-out gems among your group may not be the people you expect.

As for the others, don't be afraid to move on. In time, there will be sober friends to swap into your inner circle. Remember, it's about quality, not quantity.

Another thing that happens in time is that you will feel ready to step back into the social scene. The growing "sober curious" movement means that many bars offer plenty of choice for non-drinkers, so there's no need to nurse a lime and soda or a Diet Coke all night.

Seeing the night-time "scene" through sober eyes is fascinating. You may well find that you don't want to be out as late. You can have a couple of non-alcoholic craft beers or sparkling water if you prefer and see everybody until the point that they start arguing and repeating themselves. Then you get to go home early, get cosy, and enjoy the next day while they're gritting their teeth, full of regret.

Surely that's the best of both worlds?

Friendships provide the perfect example of how going alcohol-free leaves you with fewer relationships but better and deeper ones.

When you make it clear that you've decided where you're going in life, people will either support you on that journey or not.

It's also worth giving some thought to the friend you are, as well as the friends you have. Friendship works both ways, and there's a good chance that not drinking will make you a better friend to the people who matter.

Drunks only really make good friends with other drunks. More broadly, they're often the people who cancel at the last minute, the people who always turn up more focussed on the booze than the occasion, and the people that others fret about whether to invite to the wedding or the christening.

There may even be friends from the past who are ready to welcome you back with open arms. Perhaps you didn't actually "grow apart" from certain people. Perhaps they distanced themselves from you after one too many cancelled meet-ups or careless comments.

If you become a better quality friend, you will attract a better quality of friendships. True friendship is about turning up, being present, and being a reliable source of support. It's not about being "the wildcard" at every social event.

Friendships can become much deeper without the common ground of alcohol.

Intimacy comes from genuine friendship, not from drunkenly sharing secrets with boozy mates and then regretting you did it.

The “sober cull” is very real, but the end result is worth it. Real friends are better than “drinking friends,” even if you don’t have as many of them!

Sober Dating

Alcohol compromises your judgement, interferes with your decision making, and “causes you to be more reckless”. (NHS).

With that in mind, it seems pretty crazy to go anywhere near it when you’re going on dates! But despite the science, that’s what the vast majority of people do.

It’s understandable that people turn to alcohol in dating situations, which can provoke anxiety in even the most confident people. The trouble is, alcohol often does far more harm than good (and not just in the dating game)!

I've been on my fair share of dates where booze has made everything worse. Confidence can morph into arrogance and "chatty" into "mouthy". The truth is, I am a completely different person when drunk. Having a few beers to "help my confidence" would be enough to turn me into a louder and more foolish version of my true, sober self.

Drunk dating generally goes one of two ways: You can really like the person but show yourself at your worst and ruin it, or end up taking things further with the wrong person because the "beer goggles" become activated!

Dating also shows that paradox where alcohol is socially acceptable, yet frowned upon when you have just a little bit too much of it. Getting "too drunk" on a date is a massive red flag for potential partners.

When you step back from drinking alcohol, dating whilst boozing is one of the things that just seems....mental. Two people with impaired judgement and compromised decision-making capabilities trying to decide whether to take things further. It's a terrible idea!

If you only meet people when you (and they) are drinking, you're not meeting the real person. You're meeting somebody with heightened senses and impaired judgement when you're suffering from the same things. It's no wonder people have so many horrific dating stories.

The solution to all of this comes when you give up alcohol. But I'm not going to pretend it's easy. Going on sober dates is one of the scariest and most intimidating parts of going alcohol-free. But it's also great for building your own natural confidence.

Dating sober doesn't give you immunity from "car crash" dates. Believe me, it's still a numbers game! However, the rawness and honesty of dating without the crutch of false confidence and jacked up senses gives you a far better chance of meeting the right person. Every rejection or boring date gets you closer to honing in on what you're searching for.

You also needn't worry about your date's impression of you. You're presenting the true, unadulterated, sober version of you. That takes some guts, and the right people will notice and admire that. The people who aren't comfortable, or who think it's "boring" that you're not drinking, are certainly not the right people for you.

It doesn't really matter whether your date chooses to drink alcohol or not. However, a date is a good time to remember the quote from earlier in the chapter: "I used to walk into a room full of people and wonder if they liked me...now I look around and wonder if I like them."

If you've decided not to drink anymore, somebody who drinks "too much" on a first date should probably raise a red flag for you, too.

Once you've been on a couple of sober dates, it all becomes far less intimidating. Instead of building fake confidence with alcohol, you're building genuine confidence without it. Natural confidence is a rather attractive and appealing thing to have.

Best of all is that when you do find "the one", you'll know you made your choice with clarity and sober judgement. And that bodes well for your future.

Before we move on to the next section, a quick warning. It's especially relevant if you have a tendency towards "relationship hopping".

It's common for people to swap an alcohol dependency for a dependency on another person - and often the wrong person. Codependence is sometimes referred to as "relationship addiction". Many people drink alcohol or use drugs to fill an emptiness in themselves - one that can also be filled by a relationship.

The best advice to counter this is not to be impatient. After all, happiness is an inside job and when you find your own rhythm in life, the right person will come into your life. Jumping into any relationship for the sake of being in one isn't the recipe for long-term harmony.

With that said, long-term harmony is what we move on to next.

Do You Really Like Your Other Half?

Not everybody who decides to quit drinking is on the dating scene. Many are already in marriages and committed relationships. This can open up a whole can of worms, especially if the relationship was built on boozy foundations.

Just as many dates are fuelled by alcohol, so are many long-term relationships. And just as alcohol forms the rocky foundations of many friendships, it also forms the rocky foundations of plenty of long-term partnerships and even marriages.

The problem here is that you may find that taking alcohol away from a relationship leaves you and your partner with little or nothing in common. If you dated when drinking, got together when drinking, and then spent the weekends, yes, drinking, you may not honestly know the person you're with. And this works both ways - your partner may not honestly know you either.

It's OK, it's not a complete disaster, but deciding to go sober can create some challenges in your marriage or long-term relationship.

Of course, you WILL change when you stop drinking. But you may also find that not drinking vastly improves your relationship. Inevitably, your partner's own relationship with alcohol will play a part in how things shake out.

Perhaps your partner will decide to join in with your sober adventure. This is more common than you might expect. If they are a regular drinker, they may like the idea of having a shot at a better life. If they only drink occasionally, the thought of not drinking probably isn't a big deal to them at all so, again, they may join you for the ride.

If you and your spouse or partner do decide to go sober together, that can be a wonderful thing. You both get to experience all the benefits together: the sober glow, the weight loss, the increasing bank balance, the energy, the drive, the focus, and a whole bunch of other things we've not discussed yet - to the power of two.

These are all ingredients for a relationship that can grow and thrive - all the benefits of giving up drinking and the opportunity to enjoy them together.

But we must be realistic here.

If you've been in a relationship that's dominated by alcohol, with two people using the substance to mask emotions and ignore bigger issues, there could be some challenges ahead.

Plenty of people enjoy a fulfilling partnership where one person drinks and the other chooses not to. But, as an example, a marriage where one person has quit drinking and the other continues to drink to excess could be destined to fail.

No two partnerships are the same. If you're in a committed relationship, you will have more insight into the dynamics of that relationship than anybody else. You will probably be able to predict how much you have to worry about.

If you're a regular drinker, in a relationship with another regular drinker, it's likely that you will "grow apart" to some extent if just one of you quits. You may choose to suggest that you "quit together to stay together".

Whatever you decide, a huge positive of quitting drinking is that you become more confident and secure in yourself, with happiness that's not reliant on anything or anyone. That's a great foundation for making an existing relationship work, or for embarking on a new one.

Booze-Free Bonking

Sober sex has a lot in common with sober dating: perhaps a little terrifying at first, but far more fulfilling, enjoyable and genuine once you're used to it!

The vast majority of drinkers have at least one sexual horror story, from waking up hungover next to the wrong person to coming back from a holiday with a worrying rash. And the reality is those bad sexual decisions can have consequences that go far beyond a sense of shame and a prescription for some cream and antibiotics.

Once you understand the science, it's a struggle to think of two activities that go worse together than drinking alcohol and having sex.

First, there are the physical effects of alcohol. Booze can (and regularly does) cause erectile dysfunction. (Iliades, 2021). For regular drinkers, this can go way beyond a one-off, "don't worry, it happens to all the guys" moment, and progress to an ongoing, recurring problem.

On the female side, alcohol's diuretic and dehydrating effects can mean a lack of lubrication - the distinctly unsexy "vaginal dryness". (Healthline).

No matter what your sexual preferences are, dry vaginas and floppy dicks don't make for memorable sexual experiences. And that's before we even get to alcohol's impact on judgement and decision making.

Aside from the very real risks of unsafe sexual encounters, STIs and unplanned pregnancies, sex when drinking is fraught with risk: The risk of sleeping with somebody you'd never have gone near when sober, and the impact on your self-esteem when you have to look at yourself in the mirror the next day.

The inhibition lowering effect of alcohol is why it's so often used alongside sex. But getting used to "doing it" without alcohol is no different to getting used to the awkward first 20 minutes of a social occasion without alcohol, or the first time hitting a dancefloor sober (the latter may actually be more intimidating!).

The rewards are big too. It's a huge confidence builder to get used to having sex without being in a boozy haze. It also comes with the added benefit of knowing that you definitely want to be doing it with the person you're doing it with!

Alcohol is primarily a depressant, as we discussed earlier in the book. It's not heightening the sexual experience, it's dulling it. Having fully working genitals is handy too.

Human beings are more than capable of making bad decisions without alcohol. Quitting booze doesn't mean you're guaranteed a lifetime of perfect sexual partners and perfect sexual experiences. However, sex is more enjoyable sober, for both physical and psychological reasons.

Sober sex can help relationships to grow. When you have the courage to "leave the light on" and truly get to know your partner inside and out, you will know that being sober on a drunk planet is FAR from boring.

And, of course, sex isn't merely a way to enjoy yourself - it's also about making babies.

It turns out that booze is not at all helpful there either. Official advice for women trying to conceive is to avoid alcohol completely (Drinkaware). As few as one to five drinks per week can "reduce a woman's chances of conceiving".

Add a male drinker to the mix, and things get even worse, thanks to alcohol "lower(ing) testosterone levels and sperm quality and quantity". It's ironic that excessive drinking is viewed as a "manly" thing to do, when impotence and a low sperm count are seen as "unmanly" attributes.

If becoming a parent is your objective, alcohol may not be helping.

Parenting With Hangovers

Being a boozy parent is a life of never feeling that you're good enough.

Even if you're a "happy drunk", and never lose your temper, break promises or act irrationally, you still tend to feel like you're falling short.

Being a hungover parent is horrific. The headache, the lack of energy and the self-loathing, all combined with a noisy environment and small people who want your attention because - let's be honest - they love you more than anything in the world.

Feeling you're not giving them your best adds to the guilt and anxiety, and then your jumpiness, headache and lack of patience means you snap at them. Then you're back at the guilt part of the cycle again.

Maybe they were misbehaving and needed a telling off, but it doesn't change the fact that you feel like the world's worst human. You tell yourself, "never again".

But then, after the bedtime routine takes two and a half hours, you're so frazzled you open the wine. And the cycle begins once more.

All of this is bad enough, even if you don't drink to a degree where your actions put your children at risk of harm or distress. It can all get very serious indeed, with evidence stating that "children of alcoholics are at a significant risk for a variety of cognitive, emotional, and behavioural problems (MentalHelp.net)".

Something you hear over and over again in all the sober communities is, "I'm so much more PRESENT with my kids now."

Parenthood is incredibly hard. Children can be loud. Children can be irrational, unpredictable and argumentative. Children WILL push boundaries and rob you of your sleep and your sanity.

All parents have a unique understanding of the fact you can simultaneously love somebody more than anyone else on earth and find them profoundly, tear-your-own-hair-out infuriating!

But those who choose to be sober on a drunk planet usually come to realise that their children are part of the solution and not part of the problem. It suddenly clicks that they don't need a drink to "take the edge" off a stressful day before dealing with the kids. They find out that, sometimes, what lifts that stressful day is the hug, the unconditional love, or the random quirky outburst they would have hated to miss.

Let's not pretend this is easy. Parenting presents challenges to your finances, your mental health, your sleep, your daily routine, and your ability to relax. But, the thing is, alcohol doesn't help with ANY of those things. In fact, it makes all of those problems worse.

If drinking regularly is "living life on hard mode", parenting while drinking needs a difficulty level all of its own. It's little wonder that having children is often something that causes people to reassess their relationship with alcohol.

No child is going to grow up and tell you that you were a better parent because you were drinking all the time. All of alcohol's detrimental effects can feed into outcomes that are bad for your children - not least the risk of you being around for less of their lives.

The rewards of deciding to be a sober parent are many. Children thrive on attention, and on having parents who are fully present with them. You may even find that they put you through the ringer just a little less, in return for your greater sense of focus!

Either way, the only thing that beats being able to look in the mirror and see a good person is to look in the mirror and see a good parent. That's something money can't buy.

Sobering Family Dynamics

One final relationship dynamic we've not yet covered is the one with your wider family.

Just as some friendship groups revolve around alcohol, so do some families - brothers and sisters, parents and their adult children, and even all the aunties, uncles and cousins.

Holidays? Alcohol. Weddings? Alcohol. Anything to celebrate or commiserate? Alcohol. Many family occasions are ruined by the drunken behaviour of one or more family members. In some households, it's practically a tradition.

The damage alcohol does to extended families can compound over time. Individual incidents build into long-term resentments and get raked up over and over again. But it doesn't have to be that way.

It's unrealistic to expect your entire family to give up drinking just because you decide to. However, you may be pleasantly surprised by the example you can set. Either way, interacting with your family with clarity can only be a good thing, as can ensuring you actually turn up for events, rather than cancelling - yet again - because you're too hungover.

Even if you're part of a hard-drinking family, knowing that YOU won't be the next to create a bitter, drunken memory is liberating. It allows you to relax and enjoy your family's company. And if you're spending a few days with them, you can enjoy all of those days, not just one big night followed by three days of headaches, guilt and recrimination.

You will probably come up with some resistance from family, especially if all they have known is that occasions are centred around alcohol. You might get asked "why you can't just have one drink" but like those friends you need to assess, if your family get too pushy, just spend more time with people who don't question it.

Remember, this decision is for YOU to give up alcohol and live a life that is better than a life where alcohol was impacting negatively on it. No family member should get in the way of that or make you feel like you have let them down because you aren't conforming to their "normal".

Not only will your family learn to respect your decisions as they see a new and vastly improved version of your former self, but you will be able to turn up for your family when they need help.

Time and time again, I would cancel family events because I was too hungover or I was out on the session, yet again. Being a valued member of your family, where they know they can rely on you, trust you and ask for your help, is one of the best parts of sobriety!

All those years where Mum and Dad looked after Drunk Sean, in his many drunken states, can now be repaid through Sober Sean and his ability to be fully present and reliable.

When you drink (and drug), every weekend, you never worry about anyone around you. You never think about how much you might be impacting your loved ones, while they see you suffer, weekend after weekend. Getting sober allows you to see the hurt you caused and fix it by giving up alcohol.

Actions speak louder than words.

If you have been "missing in action" for a number of years, they will still hold their perceptions of the drunken version of you. Based on how you acted. That's normal. Their perceptions will only change through sustained action i.e. staying sober, not through anything you say to them because they have heard it all before.

The "sober glow" is something that families see more clearly than any others. They are the ones that have raised you, seen you at your best, your worst and then when you get sober. They notice the sober awakening as much as you do.

The one thing guaranteed is that quitting drinking won't make your family relationships worse. The chances are it will help them grow positively in a way you have never experienced before.

Next, we move on to the most important relationship of all: the one you have with yourself.

Chapter 4:

The Compound Effect of Being Sober

Earlier, we looked at the vicious circle of being drunk, hungover, broke, low....and then doing it all over again. It's the path I trod for years.

By the end, I was a zombie. But long before that, I became a passenger rather than a driver in my own life. Regular drinkers are great at talking - often repeatedly - about all the things they want to achieve. They're not very good at achieving them.

It's easy to kid yourself that you're "achieving" because you're making it through each year without getting fired from work. But that's doing what you must do, not what you could be doing.

Let's look at how much time you are losing to hangovers.

Hangovers Cost Time

It doesn't help that hangovers destroy potential. People don't throw themselves into new ideas and projects when hungover - they throw themselves onto the sofa.

We've already covered alcohol's various negative "feedback loops". They lead to low energy, poor physical and mental health, a scary bank balance, and non-existent self-esteem. It's a life of "living for the weekend" - and sleep-walking painfully through the rest of each week.

It gets terrifying when you add up the time you lose.

Let's say you spend just three days per week going out, planning to go out, and recovering from going out (hungover). In my case, and in many others, that's a drastic underestimation.

Those three days per week add up to 156 days each year - every year.

There's an enormous amount you can do with that time: learning, reading, exploring the world, and working on areas of your life you want to improve, such as your fitness and self-care.

Just as drinking regularly has a compound effect that makes your life worse and worse, not drinking has a compound effect that makes it better and better. Instead of feeling increasingly hollow, frustrated and glum, you begin to feel more inspired, energetic and positive.

In the introduction, I mentioned the quote that "sobriety delivers everything alcohol promised". The time you get back when you free yourself from drinking plays a huge part in making that true.

Think about how you start a new year with lots of objectives: "I want to read that book / lose that weight / do that course / learn that workout / create that art / take up yoga / explore that place". All too often, drinkers not only fail to achieve those things, but they also have to deal with the frustration and reduced self-esteem that comes from not achieving them.

Meanwhile, the non-drinkers, with the luxury of 156 or more "extra days" each year, are getting all of it done, and more.

Shortly after quitting drinking, you begin to feel better - physically, mentally and emotionally - and it continues to build with time.

A few weeks in, as most people who try Dry January will confirm, you have a new energy for life and start to realise how much more time you have without hangovers. Unfortunately, the people who celebrate the end of Dry January with a massive session (before going straight back to their old ways) don't realise that the best was yet to come.

The compound effect of choosing to be sober every day, compared to being hungover for half the week, is INCREDIBLY powerful in transforming your life. Anonymous groups talk about "just for today" and the power of just focusing your effort on being sober for 24 hours. But when you do that repeatedly for weeks, months and years, you see all the amazing achievements you have gained along the way.

The "Life Coach Effect"

The "Life Coach Effect" is something I've witnessed in the sober community. Lots of people who quit drinking go on to be life coaches, personal trainers, therapists or yoga teachers.

To begin with, I hated seeing all of those "self-righteous" people preaching about how much better life is when sober. I left plenty of AA meetings and online sober communities thinking, "what a bunch of w**kers!"

But then I started to get more sober time under my belt and started to believe in myself - for what felt like the first time in my life.

I subsequently left the corporate world, started my own business, re-trained as a life coach, qualified as a strength & conditioning coach and trained to be a counsellor and yoga instructor! I guess I'm now one of those w**kers! But, joking aside, the energy needed to qualify in all of those new careers and combine them into a business that lets me live an amazing life is all down to the power of sobriety.

When you discover something good, you want others to experience it too, especially when it's the kind of genuine contentment you spent years trying to find. That's the "Life Coach Effect" in action. My love for exercise and how it helped me change as a person, is why I get up at 5 am every morning to help others get stronger and fitter.

The reason why I mention the "Life Coach Effect" is that you see, time and time again, incredible transformations from people getting sober that leads them to wake up with purpose and drive. Something they never thought possible until they got sober.

If you are looking for a complete overhaul and want to join the growing list of sober coaches who become Personal Trainers, Life Coaches, Yoga Instructors and so on, giving up alcohol could be the missing ingredient.

While I love my job now, getting sober was difficult and transitioning careers was hard work. But when you have given up alcohol and drugs, in a world obsessed by it all, you feel as though you've acquired a "superpower". A superpower that makes you believe in yourself and that anything is possible.

The insane drive and energy you get from being consistently sober (that compound effect again) is what fuels the "Life Coach Effect" and helps create incredible transformations.

When you put an intense amount of positive energy and drive in turning an area of your life around, without hangovers and guilt getting in the way, you can transform those areas very quickly.

Life projects that looked years away, are suddenly achieved in a couple of months.

Maybe your life has got so boring, that you are willing to give anything a go. Giving up alcohol could be the kick up the arse you need to start your own transformation, whether its physical, mental, a change of career or a complete overhaul in all areas of your life.

I wouldnt be where I was, by doing it all on my own. Getting help and letting people in was a big part of my journey. This is where we go to next.

Asking For Help

If you're serious about personal growth (and with only one life, you probably should be), it's well worth thinking about seeing a therapist or at least doing some work on understanding why alcohol became such a big part of your life.

It wasn't all plain sailing when I got sober and I needed a lot of outside help to unravel why I was drinking so heavily in the first place. Being an addict isn't the answer to my problems; addiction was a temporary band-aid for deeper routed problems.

Alcohol and drugs were used to numb the pain. So when I did get sober I needed a lot of support to understand who I really was.

Alcohol blocks your emotions. Beginning to understand yourself and your emotions whilst sober can be daunting and new. Many people do what I did and embark on their adult life with alcohol as a crutch. That can mean you've not yet tried to live as an adult in a raw and "unassisted" state.

It's rather like being a newborn baby, seeking to understand the world for the very first time. That can be tough to deal with alone.
Counsellors/Therapists/Coaches can help, and so can Anonymous groups (more on those in a bit) and online communities.

Spending time in rehab and going through the 12 step programme helped me to come to terms with the fact that I'd not gone a week without drinking or drugging since the age of 15. How could I ever know who I was if my default was to use alcohol or drugs to manage my emotions?

When something became difficult, I would activate my "f**k it" button and go "out-out". Nothing ever got resolved. Instead, I swept my growing list of problems under the carpet, choosing to self-medicate with alcohol, drugs, food, gambling, and anything else I could distract myself with.

Having finally landed in rehab, after 17 years of avoiding my emotions, I was slapped in the face by the fact I had to work through them rather than carry on ignoring them. I had to build the emotional intelligence I'd neglected since my teenage years.

For me personally, regular counselling when I gave up alcohol saved my life (thanks again Patrick!). Having been a "typical" male, whose emotions were in deep space somewhere, being able to be honest and open about my life was completely transformational. It was a skill I'd never used before but the relief you feel when you tell a complete stranger how you ACTUALLY feel is amazing.

Working through challenges in your head and in your life with someone trained to help you in that particular area, has changed my outlook on coaching forever.

You will see INSANE levels of growth if you choose the right coach, whether they are a sober coach, personal trainer, counsellor, business coach, sex coach and so on. Getting sober allowed me to see the value in getting others to help, where you pay them for their experience, which ultimately saves you time, money and frustration.

Asking for help when you give up the booze might sound like an admission of weakness but I can assure you that it's the strongest action I have ever taken. You might be an emotional mess when you take away your favourite "medicine", but opening up to someone trained to guide you to a better life is certainly something I highly recommend.

Even scarier, but just as liberating, is telling a group of strangers how you feel! Attending Anonymous group meetings, I would be scared, frightened, angry, sad, happy, and that's before the meeting even started. But once the meeting took place, you really do feel a sense of serenity. The fact that you hear others going through the same challenges as you, is incredibly comforting and provides you with a sense of relief.

The 12-step programme is like a spiritual personal growth tool kit. If you need the support of the fellowship, then the 12-step programme will help you towards becoming a better person.

Going to Anonymous meetings was as much about personal growth as seeing my counsellor, personal trainer and reading up on self-development. Everything was incredibly uncomfortable but I soon realised that nothing grows in the comfort zone and all these experiences were making me more resilient as a person.

Even meeting up with new sober friends that I met on Instagram seemed a rather alien experience but one that I wouldn't have bothered with if I was hungover and not looking for a better way of life.

The reason I mention these things is that personal growth is a huge part of learning to be sober on a drunk planet. It's at once both exciting and terrifying which is a world away from the monotony of drinking, drugging, hangover, regret and repeat.

If it doesn't challenge you, it doesn't change you.

Giving up alcohol challenges you ALOT, especially on this drunk planet. But you soon build up a resistance to it and a new life you can be proud of.

Alcohol-Free Achievements

Many people planning to quit drinking worry about being "bored". Instead of feeling inspired and excited by the thought of around 156 extra days each year, they feel terrified by the prospect.

I can assure you that that feeling doesn't last. Once you start to tick off achievements, both large and small, you will soon wish you had more spare days.

Facing life head-on is scary, but living a sober life teaches you true resilience. Every time you achieve something without the "aid" of alcohol, you build a tiny extra brick of self-confidence. Those bricks build solid, real, unshakable foundations.

The more established those foundations become, the more you begin to believe in yourself, and the more willing you are to embark on the "big stuff".

All you have to do is identify things that interest you: read, take courses, listen to books on Audible - just take whatever steps you need to bring you closer to things you want. You can do literally anything.

Sure, sober life can be boring if you stubbornly refuse to do anything. But every time you open your computer, you have access to the entirety of the world's knowledge. You can, right now, learn music production, gourmet cooking, boxing, tantric sex, web design, pilates, creative writing, programming, a foreign language....the list goes on.

Once again, you have just one life. No child, when asked what they "want to be when they grow up", says a drinker.

One of the many wonderful things about quitting drinking is that you get to go back to that basic question. All of those extra days allow you to do the things you truly want to.

It may take you some time to work out what those things are, especially if you've been so absorbed in the drinking lifestyle that you've forgotten how to dream. But that's OK.

It's exciting - and all of the mental and physical health benefits of being booze-free give you the energy and clarity to feel that excitement. Yet again, it's another feedback loop, but a really rewarding one.

Personal growth means different things to different people, but it's almost certain that - in time - it will boil down to specific goals.

When I managed to stay clean and sober, I had just one goal: to get myself out of my corporate setting and find a job that I actually liked! I noticed a real "snowball effect" after that, with bigger, better and more ambitious goals. I can assure you it never gets boring.

When you start achieving goals, nothing can stop the new virtuous circle. More goals ticked off means more confidence, which means you're more likely to try (and succeed) at the next thing. It's truly mind-blowing when you can look back at a single year, having achieved a whole bunch of plans that you'd spent over a decade making zero progress on.

Let's turn briefly back to the alternative, which we ran through at the start of this book: a circle of nights out, hangovers, low moods, neglected plans and abandoned dreams.

You have a choice of which circle you want to continue in, and that takes us back to something I said right at the start: Giving up drinking doesn't mean giving up something good - it's simply swapping one kind of life for a better one. And you don't meet people in sobriety who wish for their old life back.

In the next chapter, we continue to talk about personal growth, this time on the spiritual side.

We've already covered having better health, more money, better relationships and more success, but what if you could also experience happiness on a deeper level than ever before? And what if that was on offer to you whether or not you believe in any kind of God or religion?

It's time to talk about spirituality.

Chapter 5:

The Sober Awakening

Living for the weekend makes for a grim existence. But it's an existence many people fall into and settle for.

Life can get very repetitive, especially if you're working in a job you don't enjoy, sticking with it purely because you can turn up hungover and still get paid. A life designed around "making it through" the day or the week, until you can have a beer or a glass of wine, is soulless and empty.

It's important not to blame yourself if that's what your life looks like. We're all conditioned to think it's normal, hence "happy hour" and "wine o'clock". But there are 365 days in a year, and only

104 of them are weekend days. Is it not worth learning to relish the other 261?

My life during the 12 years I spent in the corporate world was boring and predictable: Get up, go to work, have lunch, watch the clock run down from 2 pm till 5 pm (when time appeared to almost stop), and then make a quick exit - either home or to a bar.

My main aims were to get through the day having done some work and to get through the year having done enough to get paid a bonus.

That bonus paid for some "things", which did nothing to nourish my soul. They just allowed me to pretend I was momentarily happy with my life. It was a very soulless existence. I used alcohol and drugs to numb the pain of how boring and soulless it actually was.

We're conditioned to believe that material things (like those purchased with my annual bonus) can fill the void. But if that were true, there wouldn't be any unhappy rich people!

The "living for the weekend" lifestyle is the same as the "rat race" lifestyle. There's little genuine difference between somebody grafting on minimum wage to pay for a couple of nights in their local pub and a stockbroker working all week and "celebrating" with champagne, caviar and cocaine. It comes down to little more than pricier drugs and glitzier venues.

I did my time in the corporate world. But after a couple of years of sobriety, I felt a strong urge to move on to something different. I was in a position where I could get the "things:" the bigger house, the bigger car. All I needed to do was work longer hours, get more stressed, and burn myself out every few months.

But however much of it I did, the work still left me feeling empty. Giving up alcohol allowed me to see the light and understand that the corporate world didn't feed my soul.

What is Spirituality?

Let's take a look at the dictionary definition of spirituality:

Spirituality: "the quality of being concerned with the human spirit or soul as opposed to material or physical things (Oxford Languages)".

Note that the definition says nothing about any God. Whether you're a devout believer or an atheist, you have a soul that is either nourished or neglected. And neither alcohol nor material things feed the soul.

The "work hard, play hard" lifestyle that so many people pride themselves on doesn't nourish the soul. It comes down to something as simple as the fact that money can't buy happiness - and neither can bigger houses, faster cars and expensive holidays.

"Work hard, play hard" is the perfect lifestyle for people who want to burn themselves out and live increasingly materialistic lives. None of it has any correlation with happiness and contentment.

Alcohol has a stronger connection to all of this than it might initially appear. Alcohol (and other drugs) can make you a passive participant in the rat race. If Monday to Friday are about doing the job and making money, and Saturday and Sunday are about dulling and forgetting the monotony of it all, how is anything going to change?

Giving up alcohol creates the space for things to change. It breaks the cycle and allows you to think about what "being concerned with the human spirit or soul" could mean for you - with or without a God.

A balanced and contented life requires you to think about three things: mind, body and soul. You can think of them as three cups you need to keep full.

All too often, people think only about the first two cups. They concentrate on trying to look good and "be the best" (mind and body) and forget all about the soul. Materialism is a big part of this, too.

Many people (wrongly) assume that looking and being "the best" is about the size of the house, the job title, or where they go on holiday.

Part of becoming sober on a drunk planet is waking up to this and realising that the third cup is equally important. It doesn't matter how many zeroes you have on your bank balance if you're numb to the beauty of the world around you and are neglecting your soul. You will still be miserable.

Spirituality means different things to different people. For some, it's all about connecting with nature. For others, it's about a constant quest for learning and self-improvement. Some people feed their soul by volunteering, helping others and campaigning about things they care about. Others find profound peace in activities like yoga and meditation. And, yes, for some, it's about religion.

Spiritual Solutions For Soulless Existences

Now is a good moment to speak a little about Alcoholics Anonymous and other 12-step programmes. I should emphasise that AA doesn't appeal to everybody, but - for many - it plays a huge part in the spiritual side of getting sober.

The 12 steps were truly transformative for me and changed my perspective on life. It's no exaggeration to describe it as a spiritual awakening.

Alcoholics Anonymous was started in 1935 by a stockbroker (Bill Wilson) and a surgeon (Dr Bob Smith). Both had developed a serious dependence on alcohol.

Since the 12 step programme that formed the basis of AA's "spiritual approach to recovery", it has expanded into all kinds of other addictions. We now have Cocaine Anonymous, Narcotics Anonymous, Sex Addicts Anonymous, Overeaters

Anonymous, Gamblers Anonymous and many more.

The "spiritual" nature of the 12 step programme does cause some misunderstandings. Mentions of "God" and a "higher power" lead some people to (incorrectly) see AA as a religious group. Alcoholics Anonymous themselves emphasise that this is not the case. (Alcoholics Anonymous).

While AA "has its origins in a Christian group," the program is spiritual and not religious. Plenty of diverse individuals, including Buddhists, atheists and agnostics, take part in (and benefit hugely from) 12 step programmes.

The 12 steps lead you through - among other things - admitting you have a problem, having faith in a "power greater than yourself", taking a moral inventory, righting your wrongs, and helping others going through similar journeys.

Millions of people enjoy the process of "working the steps" methodically. However, there's no obligation to do that. As per AA's own guidelines, "newcomers are not asked to accept or follow these Twelve Steps in their entirety if they feel unwilling or unable to do so."

If you feel f**ked and feel that your soul needs a reboot, 12 step programmes have helped millions of people around the world. If you're truly f**ked, like I was, you should be willing to give anything a try. Anonymous groups are a great place to do some soul-searching.

There's absolutely nothing stopping you from testing the water. Online meetings are widespread, so you can do so without even leaving your home, if you prefer. If you want greater insight into the 12-step programme, Russell Brand's "Recovery" provides a great introduction to each of the 12 steps.

While the whole "higher power" thing is a struggle for some, it completely changed how I viewed the world.

I will explain briefly what "higher power" means to me because it has saved me a lot of stress and allowed me to grow as a person.

Acknowledging a "higher power" means understanding that you can only control what you can actually control. Anything outside of that needs to be left to a "higher power", in whatever form that takes for you. It could mean fate, God, the universe, or any interpretation you choose. It could be as straightforward as acknowledging that there's a whole bunch of stuff you personally have no power over.

Failing to accept that there's a higher power leads you to try to control situations that are out of your control. This can cause nothing other than frustration and anger since you have no power over the final outcome. It's simply "banging your head against a brick wall".

Many people assume "higher power" means God. While that is what the founders of Alcoholics Anonymous had in mind originally, the organisation has evolved. People from all walks of life take part, and they have all kinds of different beliefs. So don't let that misapprehension put you off from giving the 12 steps a go.

Alcohol and drugs changed the person I was. Sober Sean is not the same person as Drunk Sean. The 12 steps enabled me to realise that and recognise my patterns. Most importantly, they allowed me to forgive myself and move beyond that old self.

Other people forgave me too. Daunting though it felt to begin with, apologising to the people I'd hurt (the ninth step) was the most rewarding part of all, and key to moving forward into my new life. I won't, however, try to deny that it was one of the scariest things I've ever done.

There's no other way to describe it than as a spiritual moment. Everything I learned when completing the 12 steps finally made "the penny drop", and helped me understand my addiction and how alcohol was linked to all my bad decisions.

As I said, the 12 steps aren't for everyone - but they were a huge part of my own journey. Your journey needn't be the same as mine.

There are plenty of other lessons you can learn away from 12 step programmes. Perhaps you will find your soul in music, in charitable work, or in yoga and meditation.

Going back to what we said at the start of this chapter, you're going to free up a whole bunch of time to discover what makes your spirit sing, so why not try everything that sparks your interest?

There were a couple of big lessons I learned, away from the structure of Anonymous groups: Something just as transformative as the 12 steps was learning about the role of the ego, and the part it plays in your life.

I highly recommend reading (or listening to) "A New Earth", by Eckhart Tolle - a book that I place firmly in my "life-changing" category.

Anybody who's walked down a rowdy high street on a Friday night will know that alcohol and ego don't always make for a great mix. Alcohol can vastly inflate the ego, and consuming it regularly - especially on a drunk and materialistic planet - can quickly send things spinning out of control.

Getting sober, and absorbing that book, allowed me to finally understand the role of my ego, and begin to work with it in a healthy way, rather than letting it control my life.

Learning the power of being present (essentially "living in the moment") was also a huge part of my sobriety journey.

When you regularly drink or take drugs, it's practically impossible to live in the moment. This is ironic, given how much we convince ourselves that's what "partying" is all about.

In reality, you spend a lot of time in the past, "What did I do? What did I say? How much did I spend?" and in the future, "How am I going to get through work with this hangover? How will I tell the landlord I've spent the rent? What time can I start drinking again?".

Using alcohol and drugs made my life constantly chaotic, and you can't be present in chaos. My mind was constantly worrying about the past and future. That's an exhausting way to live.

Getting sober allowed me to learn about being present - not looking back or forward, merely enjoying the now.

You'll have no problem finding lots of material on mindfulness and being present. It's a fashionable subject, and it deserves its popularity because it's hugely powerful when you master it. I highly recommend Eckhart Tolle's "The Power of Now", another book that changed my life and allowed my mind to finally stop overthinking.

I can't talk about spirituality without a mention of yoga and meditation, both of which are widely seen as spiritual practices.

Yoga is very much a "mind, body and spirit" practice, said to "create mental clarity and calmness, increase body awareness, relieve chronic stress patterns, relax the mind, centre attention and sharpen concentration". (American Osteopathic Association).

Like attending Alcoholics Anonymous, doing yoga is probably something that either inspires you or makes you think, "nope, no chance". But it's worth knowing that an estimated 300 million people practice yoga worldwide. (The Good Body). It seems unlikely that all those individuals are doing it and getting nothing out of it.

The reason why people do yoga, isn't just to look great and move into stupidly named poses such as pigeon, dolphin or happy baby. It's incredibly cleansing for your mind too.

Focusing on your yoga practice, while trying your best to hold those poses and move through your flow, means your mind is not thinking about other things. You can only concentrate on the present moment. That involves trying not to fall over, pull a muscle or worse, fart in a crowded yoga studio.

If you have never tried it, give yoga a go because you can help your mind, body and soul all at once!

Once again, not drinking gives you lots of time to try these things out and the mental clarity to approach them with an open mind.

The same applies to meditation. Again, it's a spiritual practice that hundreds of millions of people enjoy. Even if you're not (yet) sold on the soulful side of things, the 84% of people who practise meditation "to reduce stress and anxiety" can't all be wasting their time. (FinancesOnline).

Nobody's saying you have to do any of these things. Your spiritual journey is yours alone. But these are things that have not just worked for me but are widely praised by those who get sober.

It's not a binary choice. It's not about either being a party animal or swapping it all for a yoga mat and wardrobe full of lycra. Nor is it about turning your back on money and status and becoming a "spiritual being".

Remember those three cups labelled "mind," "body" and "soul". It doesn't matter how you choose to fill them. And there's nothing wrong with aspiring to be rich and fit or a powerful CEO with a nourished soul!

Just remember not to neglect that third cup.

While you may be inspired by some of the things I did to "fill that cup", part of the fun of sobriety is working out what does it for you. Maybe it could be running marathons, buying some turntables and learning to DJ, or volunteering at an animal shelter.

Finding out what "moves you" in a life free from alcohol and drugs can be a lot of fun. And fun is what we talk about next. You have lots of it to come.

Chapter 6:

Sober NOT Boring

Going out drinking is a pretty weird kind of fun.

You go out and drink (because, well, that's what people do), but the price of that big night out is two or three days of feeling rough - perhaps longer, if you're advancing in years. You also, as we've already discussed, have to deal with the financial cost of that night out.

So, that "good night out" is defined by spending a load of money, only remembering patches of the evening, and then feeling like sh*t (mentally and physically) for days after.

That's supposed to be FUN?!

The trouble is, we live on a drunk planet. Using alcohol to have fun is a societal thing. We live in a world with a drinking "culture" (although "culture" seems like a rather grand word for something so daft).

Society expects you to have "fun" by going out and drinking. Billions are spent on alcohol advertising to keep the "culture" thriving.

It's not your fault if you don't understand how to have fun without alcohol. Boozing is seen as something you're finally allowed to do when you reach adulthood. We're practically conditioned to forget the thousands of other ways of enjoying ourselves.

The conditioning runs deep, and it's why not drinking is sometimes seen as "boring". Some people may even call you "boring" if you decide to stop conforming to the drinking culture. (We've already covered what to do about that in the chapter on relationships).

To begin with, alcohol does provide a little bit of superficial fun. It lowers your inhibitions and gives you a boost of confidence. You may even like the taste of it (although I never really did).

The trouble is that the fun stops, and when it stops it really stops: blackouts, cripplingly expensive nights out, battered mental and physical health, and the impact of all the bad decisions that go with drinking - such as drug-taking, gambling, promiscuity and awful food.

The truly crazy part is that millions of people carry on drinking, even when they've seen and lived through those impacts time and time again.

It shows just how ingrained the culture is. We come to accept that fun has all of those undesirable consequences - and potentially far worse ones. We all know about Amy Winehouse, Oliver Reed, Billie Holiday, Avicci, Heath Ledger and many more. The end-game is there for us to see - but we carry on anyway.

Fortunately, sober fun doesn't have those consequences.

Redefining "Fun"

Just as quitting drinking frees up masses of time to feed your soul, it frees up time for fun too. Often, the two things merge. If fun, for you, means flying to an exciting destination and climbing a mountain, chances are that will nourish your spirit too.

But not everything you do has to have a spiritual point. It's your time - so do exactly as you please with it.

As with so many of the benefits of quitting drinking, it's not only about the time and money you save from the drinking itself. Hangovers aren't fun. Weekends can be about actually having the fun rather than sleeping it off.

As your "sober time" builds, so too does your confidence. Things that seem intimidating when you're shaky, aching and smelling like a pub aren't intimidating when you've woken up fresh and know you'd pass a breathalyser test. Maybe you can book the skydive, strap yourself to a snowboard, or pluck up the courage to go to that Muay Thai class.

When you start branching out and doing these things, you quickly realise that there are many other people doing them too. You begin to notice that there's a whole parallel world of other people - who weren't out last night and aren't nursing hangovers.

As soon as you have your first "brilliant day" or "great night" that didn't involve a drop of alcohol, you begin to understand that that whole world is open to you. It's exciting, and it further boosts your confidence.

Natural confidence is worlds apart from the short-lived, artificial confidence you get from a few shots or a couple of lines of cocaine. You get to think about what you really fancy doing, go out and do it, and go home whenever you want.

That leads us neatly on to sober socialising, something that every ex-drinker must learn to navigate on a drunk planet.

Sober Socialising, Hobbies & Holidays

Let's start with a huge positive: an exciting world of no and low alcohol drinks has emerged in the past five years. It's an industry now worth nearly US$10 Billion - and growing. (IWSR).

What this means is that you can still have a good night out with plenty of "grown-up" drinks: alcohol-free craft beers, cocktails and even some palatable 0% wines. You can go out with people who choose to drink, have four or five drinks with them, and still be up first thing for whatever fun activity you have planned.

Equally, if you don't want to drink alcohol-related drinks, like me, there is nothing more powerful, than drinking a glass of water.

The increasing popularity of the "sober curious" movement means that you may not even find yourself explaining your reasons for not drinking. People may not notice. But being realistic, you probably will have "the conversation" plenty of times. It gets easier on each occasion, and ultimately people can either accept your desire for a better life or not. If you're not comfortable talking about why you are giving up alcohol just yet, use something like, "I'm training for the next Olympics" or "I can't handle another psychotic outburst in public again". The latter is likely to stop any further questions as well.

If you do socialise with people who are drinking, you may decide to leave earlier than them or to skip the club. Don't fret. They probably won't care at the time, and by the time they're nursing a hangover, the only feeling they will have is one of envy for not making the same choices as you!

While they're bathing in self-regret and piecing together the evening before, you can be out and enjoying whatever pastimes, sports and hobbies make you happy. These can be things that appealed to you before you started drinking or something entirely new.

If, for example, you played a sport or had a hobby before you started spending most weekends drunk or hungover, take it up again and try it sober. You'll likely find you're much better at it!

You can do whatever you want: yoga, meditation, knitting, reading, developing a side hustle, starting a business, writing a novel, learning an instrument, building new friendships. When you decide to stay sober on a drunk planet, you get to redefine what fun means and start living life on your terms, not your friends, family, workmates or by societal "norms".

Giving up alcohol allows you to become the driver and not the passenger on your own journey to having fun.

If improved fitness is a part of your plan, you will find out the gym is actually open on Saturdays and Sundays (a fact that passes many regular drinkers by!). Being sober allows you to spend more time on exercise, burn more calories and really benefit from your newfound zest for life.

There's no obligation to make fitness one of your new hobbies when you quit drinking. However, finding regular exercise that you enjoy can be one of the best things about sobriety. There are plenty of choices, so you're sure to find something that appeals, and it helps to maximise the feeling of wellbeing.

Once you begin to understand the true meaning of self-care, you see what "relaxing" truly means. What it doesn't mean is going out drinking and then feeling like crap for the next few days.

That's not fun. Fun is doing the things you enjoy and are passionate about, without having to pay for them physically, emotionally and mentally.

Another enjoyable part of being sober is taking sober holidays. Yes, they're very different, but imagine going on holiday and coming back re energised and with a new enthusiasm for life - rather than being broke, tired and needing another holiday to get over it all.

Again, for most people, drinking alcohol doesn't equal true relaxation. Being hungover, skint and full of regret isn't relaxing. "Writing off" one or more days of a long-awaited holiday because you're cowering in your hotel room feeling sick and headachey is a terrible way to spend your time off.

I've been on plenty of holidays, but most were "wasted" in more ways than one! I've done lots of "18-30" style trips, including those to Ibiza, Spring Break in Cancun and the Greek islands. If you haven't drunk a fishbowl of lethal cocktail and had the ten free shots that came with it, count yourself as lucky.

Regardless of the destination, I'd repeat the same pattern. I'd go on a "massive one" on the first night and be violently sick thanks to my inability to stomach too much alcohol. I'd then spend the remaining days alternating between suffering and trying to do it all again. Looking back to those alcohol-fuelled holidays, being hungover for 7-days wasn't much "fun".

Making the most of every moment is much better. Exploring the local sites is a better use of time than searching for an open pharmacy to buy some painkillers. Holiday time is precious time, whether it's time by yourself or time with your nearest and dearest. Wasting it on hangovers is a bit tragic.

A holiday can be anything you want it to be: time to completely switch off and work through a pile of books, time to discover every hidden corner of a new city or time to indulge in hobbies and try new things. If all a holiday is time to hammer booze and drugs, you may as well stay at home.

Learning to have sober fun can take some time. The people you surround yourself with can play a big part in how easy it is. Joining some kind of sober community is a great way to do fun things with like-minded people.

There are plenty of communities out there where you can find your tribe. If you're an Instagram fan, it's well worth following related hashtags and accounts - for ideas and inspiration, and perhaps even to find some people on your wavelength.

As a starting point, look out for anyone with a username like sober(name) or a #sober(something) hashtag. If you want to remain anonymous to your drinking pals, then just start up your own sober account.

Facebook has plenty of online groups as well if Instagram is a bit too much and more and more sober communities are popping up as increasing numbers of people become sober on a drunk planet.

I'm going to end this chapter by reemphasising two things:

1. You can have a huge amount of fun when you're sober.

2. Being sober does NOT mean that any aspect of your life will be boring.

I can honestly say that I've never met anybody who has regretted turning sober. A life filled with hobbies, passions and interests is rewarding and - yes - fun.

If you're in any doubt about this, try to think back to your childhood, before a drop of alcohol had passed your lips. Almost certainly, you will have had hobbies, interests, and things you would have loved to try doing.

As a sober adult, you have the time, the freedom and the money to do them all. If that's not fun, I don't know what is!

Next, we talk about something that - to many - isn't much fun at all: business and careers. One of the many exciting things about living a sober existence is that you can make your working life something you enjoy rather than endure.

Imagine enjoying the 261 weekdays of each year as well as making the most of every single weekend. It's yet another life-changing benefit of giving up alcohol.

Chapter 7:

The Sober Worker

There are some horrifying statistics out there around how many people hate (or merely tolerate) their jobs. One global poll found that 85% of people are "not engaged" by their work (Clifton, 2017).

There have been many studies around this, and while not all of them create such a staggering headline, most show that a solid majority of people are dissatisfied with their working lives.

However you look at it, that's pretty depressing. Accounting for holidays and weekends, most of us spend well over 200 days working each year. It's one hell of a waste of your adult life if you're miserable for those days.

Why do so many people tolerate a life like that? A big part of it is that we live on a drunk planet.

A never-ending cycle of alcohol-fuelled weekends followed by lethargic, hungover weeks robs you of the ability to make the best use of your working time.

In the chapter on spirituality, we talked about the "work hard, play hard" lifestyle, also known as the "rat race". Not only is it the cultural norm for many, but it's also a trap.

If you go out every weekend and live paycheck to paycheck, you have little option but to tolerate the job you're in. "Rising up the ranks" doesn't solve the problem, because your lifestyle tends to expand to match your salary.

There are plenty of people out there on huge salaries who are still stuck in jobs they hate - due to things like big mortgages, car payments and school fees. That's what happens when you live a materialistic life and are always chasing after the next "thing".

The rat race still traps people who don't drink alcohol. If you are a regular drinker, you're not giving yourself even a tiny chance - least of all for all the financial reasons discussed earlier in the book.

Here's what happens when you try to juggle a job with a party lifestyle: You may well hate the job, but you tolerate it. You spend the weekends bitching and moaning about work, passionately believing that you're "worth more to the business" and that your bonus should be higher.

But then Monday comes around and you're back at your desk. You're far too jaded and hungover to do anything other than stay on the hamster wheel. You need the money and they're paying you to endure your hangover on a weekday, so it can't be all bad, right?

It IS bad. It's especially bad if you allow years to pass like that. That's what I did, and it's what many others do too.

Ready to break the cycle? Once again, the powerful answer is to give up alcohol.

Alcohol And Work - The Recipe For Disaster

The simple fact is that alcohol and "climbing the ladder" don't mix. That's not to say you won't steadily progress, or that there aren't toxic workplaces where people do manage to get ahead and get drunk in parallel. But as a general rule, alternating between being drunk and being hungover is not the route to smashing your career goals.

Being the office "legend" is not the same as being the office superstar. Many a career path is destroyed by drunken behaviour on work nights out. Weekends of anxiety spent worrying about getting fired are bad enough, but the long-term damage is even worse. Repeated stupidity on nights out earns you nothing other than a reputation, and will almost certainly slow down your progression.

My first work night out in the finance world was heralded as a "low key" office quiz. Unfortunately, I attended it with the anxiety of being the new guy and an inability to stop drinking.

By the end of the night, I'd found myself immersed in a rubbish bin outside the pub. No taxi would take me home because I was too wrecked. Luckily an old school friend worked behind the bar and somehow got me home to my very embarrassed parents (Thank you Karl!).

This was just the first day of my 12-year career in the corporate world!

Lots of people go to work, do nothing more than "go through the motions", and still feel like they're being robbed of the progression they "deserve". I did that for years. I also had no problem finding other colleagues to moan to about it.

Many workplaces have a culture where people do this night after night. They keep pubs and bars in business while they drink and complain about the firm. Usually, the people who are actually getting the promotions aren't in the bar with them - certainly not as regularly.

Perhaps you have much in common with your "happy hour crew" of co-workers. But, being realistic, it's more likely your main shared interests are partying and complaining about the boss, or about the company "culture".

While you bounce from bar to club to office and back again, you see other people shooting past you in their careers. They're winning promotions and being given additional responsibility or meeting their sales targets with relative ease. You feel frustrated because they make it look so easy.

If this resonates, and you're a regular drinker, picture a life where you never have a single hangover. Imagine how much that changes things.

Rocket Launch Your Career

It starts with the simple stuff. When you arrive promptly in the mornings looking fresh, instead of screeching in at 9.05 am looking and smelling stale, people do notice.

It feels good too. The days that begin that way are usually the better days, as you'll already know from those occasional mornings when you do have your sh*t together. When you don't drink at all, and never run the risk of a hangover, you have far more good working days than bad. It's as simple as that.

Then it all begins to compound - in a good way.

Remember that mental clarity and super-fast cognition you get as a result of giving up alcohol? It builds over time and transforms how you perform at work. Your memory, your power of reasoning, and your ability to process information all improve notably (Renewal Lodge, 2019).

You quickly go from "office sloth" to "office ninja!".

As your weeks of sobriety build to months and years, everything starts to snowball. The people that matter notice the change in you. You can still be the black sheep at the office parties, but standing out because you're sober is far more appealing than standing out because you vomited all over your boss.

As your performance and reliability begins to speak for itself, you also gain the confidence to speak out for yourself. Having genuine faith in your abilities can translate to putting yourself forward for promotions or extra responsibilities, or looking out for something new and different, bigger and better.

That could include deciding to start a business and working for yourself. So far in this chapter, we’ve worked on the assumption that you have an employee position - working for somebody else. That’s not the case for everyone.

Here in the UK, around 15% of workers are self-employed - and that figure is increasing (Gov.uk, 2021).

It’s worth noting, at this point, that plenty of people run their own businesses, drink too much, and participate in that same work hard, play hard rat-race. If you're reading this as somebody who already runs a business, I can assure you that choosing to quit drinking can still vastly improve your performance and your prospects.

It's perfectly possible to be self-employed, and still, be "going through the motions" and living for the weekend. You may feel like you're "holding it down" if you're keeping a business afloat, but a drunk or hungover business owner makes all the same mistakes as a drunk or hungover employee. In some cases, the consequences can be worse, because there's nobody to manage you and ensure you get things done.

Sure, you may not have managers who notice you're hungover, but you have clients instead. They too, notice things like poor punctuality, lack of focus, and beer breath.

As we've established, drinking regularly destroys your confidence and cognitive function. This can mean you don't have the courage to market yourself boldly, or the clarity to pitch for a complicated, high-earning bit of business. Drinking kills your motivation, leaving you content to do what you have to do, rather than what you're truly capable of.

Quitting drinking gives you the time, energy and confidence to build a new business of your own, or to redouble your efforts with your existing ventures.

There are two routes out of being one of the miserable majority of people who dread Monday morning. They're both open to you (and are achievable) in sobriety. Either you can begin to excel as an employee, climbing the ranks and reaping the benefits, or you can decide to branch out on your own.

Once you remove the alcohol, there is a chance you'll discover - as I did - that you hate your corporate job. Thankfully, sobriety gives you the power to consciously choose a better role, or to finally start your dream business.

A recent survey showed that 62% of people want to start businesses of their own (Vista, 2018). Far fewer people actually do it, often due to a lack of time, confidence or money.

It's good news that time, confidence, and money are all things that you gain when you stop drinking!

Starting a business is never easy, but the surefire way to make it impossibly difficult is to be hungover and broke, with a brain that never works at full capacity. When you're firing on all cylinders, with radical clarity and a high level of resilience, anything is possible.

Deciding to give up alcohol provides nothing but good news for your business and career prospects. In sober communities, you constantly see people starting businesses they've long dreamed of, winning big promotions, and surprising themselves by achieving goals they once convinced themselves were unattainable.

Don't waste your working life doing a job you hate. Dare to dream. Waking up fresh and hangover-free is always a great feeling. Waking up on Monday morning feeling inspired and enthusiastic about making your living is better still.

Living only for the weekend is a tragic waste. The larger majority of your life is the rest of the time. You owe it to yourself to enjoy that too.

Chapter 8:

The Drunk Planet

We've talked about your health, your relationships, your soul, your career, and a wealth of other things that improve and transform when you stop drinking.

However, the fact still remains that we live on a drunk planet. And that doesn't magically change just because you do.

More and more people are opting for a sober lifestyle, but we still have a society that seems to "run on alcohol". The conditioning runs deep, so it's inevitable that you will continue to find yourself in environments where everything revolves around booze.

How many times have you heard the saying "don't trust people who don't drink alcohol" or "I use to think drinking was bad for me, so I gave up thinking". This planet is completely sh*t faced when it comes to understanding how dangerous alcohol can actually be.

Ultimately, you have to adapt to being alcohol-free in those environments or find different environments that are more compatible with the transformed version of you. The good news is that those environments do exist - but you may need to do some groundwork to find them.

In this final chapter, we look at the societal conditioning that created this drunk planet. As well as teaching you how to thrive in sobriety, it will also likely provide some reassurance. If you've found yourself stuck in an unhealthy feedback loop until now, it's really not your fault. The odds were stacked against you from the start.

There's a saying that "if you hang around the barbershop for long enough, sooner or later, you are going to get a haircut."

Similarly, if you hang around pubs and bars long enough, sooner or later, you'll get drunk. And if you're curious and prone to temptation, drugs will probably find you too. They're everywhere (and I mean everywhere).

A more accurate description is if you hang around pubs and bars long enough, you'll get drunk/high, regret it for the next day, week, month or year, be broke, feel ill, order takeaway food, miss the gym for the next week, make mistakes at work, and feel depressed, anxious and soulless.

The really crazy thing is that millions of people do that all the time, and then frame it as a "good night out". It's what you do, it's what everyone does. It's considered "normal".

In a world where pubs and bars are the default places for adult "fun" and "relaxation", it's no wonder people end up in an unhealthy cycle. That cycle got hold of me for 17 years.

That societal conditioning has a lot to answer for.

You almost feel obliged to call it a "good night out". It's what's expected of you. The internet is littered with memes and in-jokes about hangovers and drunken behaviour.

But if you actually break down what that "good night out" involved, and how you felt afterwards, was it really good? Probably not.

Let's look at a few scenarios around booze culture, and how it is such a fundamental part of daily life. After that, we will look at how to do things in a more evolved, healthy and rewarding way.

Let's Get Sh*t Faced

I spent three years at university and got "sh*t faced" almost every day. I'd often throw up after a night out and hardly remember any of it - but this was considered "normal". It was part of the university "experience" and, yes, along with many others, I convinced myself - at the time - that it was "fun".

Blackouts, excessive vomiting and idiotic behaviour shouldn't be viewed as normal - at any age. But, as we've clearly established, we live on a drunk planet. In the UK, and many other countries, getting drunk and "enjoying yourself", is what you're supposed to do when you're "young, wild and free".

Nowadays, when people ask me if I had fun at university, I am hesitant to say "yes". Blackouts, vomiting, debt and a 2:1 in Business Management is hardly worth writing about compared to my sober achievements.

I don't want to sound like a sober bore here, so I will acknowledge that student life taught me valuable life skills around socialising with people. But it all revolved around alcohol (and drugs). Even the sports days on Wednesdays were followed up that night with drunken "Athletic Union" nights!

That pattern of getting drunk after playing sport has always been around. A pattern you can see at rugby clubs, hockey clubs, rowing clubs, running clubs, football clubs, golf clubs, cricket clubs, tennis clubs, bowls clubs, and the list goes on.

We haven't even touched on the crazy drinking 'initiations' that go on at some of these 'sports' clubs. Apparently excessively drinking out of a dirty old boot while running around a field butt naked is a form of acceptance.

In my second year at university, I was voted in as a "Week One Rep". My role was to look after freshers for the first week of their university life. The job was all about getting those new arrivals as drunk as possible for seven nights in a row. All of which was endorsed by the University.

If proof were needed that booze culture is truly ingrained in universities, the "Week One Rep" role is supposedly one of the most sought-after in student life. These rituals and rites of passage present booze as some all-encompassing "elixir of life", and generation after generation of students hit early adulthood being taught that's normal.

University is just one environment where alcohol culture is endemic. There are plenty more, including boozed-up holidays.

If you grew up in the UK, then you might have heard of 18-30's style holidays. Even better still, you might have gone on one and still be regretting that one-night stand or those sex games that you were made to take part in!

British people love going abroad, getting sh*t faced every night, having food at the local Irish pub and then going back home to do it all again in a much colder climate. This was how I spent my holidays from the age of 17-25.

The culture around holidays and excessive boozing was so bad, we actually had successful travel companies making money out of it! People would endure a week of mindless drinking, vomiting, catching multiple STIs, crashing rented scooters, eating McDonald's and come home saying that was "fun".

Even when I went to Vegas, Ibiza and Cancun for what I thought was "maturing" holidays, the booze kept flowing and the drugs became a bigger part of the experience. As I got older, the hangovers were getting worse and the holidays felt more and more of a struggle.

Tired of the British cultural holidays, we decided to go to Cancun for the American style "Spring Break". We thought it might be an easier few weeks away but it turns out, Americans drink just as much as we do!

The worst part of the trip is that we went for two full weeks. I was almost 30 by this time and my liver was on the verge of nuclear fallout after just two days.

The conclusion was, it doesn't matter where you go, the booze-fuelled holiday culture is a global thing! Yes, I had fun on these holidays, but what I realise now, is that I couldn't drink like everyone else. The vomiting, blackouts, doing stupid sh*t, all followed me wherever I went and it was anything but relaxing.

Now let's have a look at another example of alcohol-fuelled culture. The workplace.

The world of manual labour has a heavy drink and drug culture. Once again it formed due to generations of people doing the same things. It's considered "normal" to finish a job at 3 pm, then head to the pub to spend most of the day's wages on alcohol (and possibly drugs too).

Turning up the next day hungover is expected and widely accepted. The circle of work - drink - hangover - repeat is nothing more than day-to-day "normal" life for many people.

It's the same in much of the corporate world. In fact, for many, entering that environment simply provides a way to continue and build on the habits learned in university.

Corporate teams drink to celebrate wins (and commiserate losses). They drink for birthdays, to welcome new starters, or to say farewell to people leaving. There are conferences, team drinks, boozy client lunches, "away days" and team-building events.

Not all offices are the same, but much of the above usually applies. Some industries are particularly "hardcore". The world of advertising has long had a reputation for being extremely boozy. Some firms reportedly provide access to rehab facilities due to the "nature of the job".

Corporate drinking culture was a disaster for me. When you have the kind of relationship with alcohol that I had, constant access to it made it very difficult to get ahead. Alcohol brings out the worst in me, and I often felt that I was "walking on eggshells" around everybody with the power to fire me.

It's nonsensical that the use of alcohol is so widely encouraged, yet overindulgence remains taboo and frowned upon. But on the drunk planet, everybody is expected to walk an incredibly delicate line - drink to fit in, but always the exact amount not to overstep the mark and do something foolish. That's not really feasible with an addictive drug that compromises your judgement!

If you want to see how widespread this problem is, check out these statistics around work Christmas parties: A survey found that 89% of people in the UK acknowledged getting drunk at these events, with 65% saying their "behaviour was affected in a negative way". 45% admitted to "making a fool of themselves", and a rather staggering 9% had been fired or disciplined (Roberts, 2018).

Quite aside from the nearly one in ten people losing their jobs as a result of the main annual work night out, those figures demonstrate that an awful lot of workers regret the things they do after a few drinks. It seems likely that across the world, millions of people destroy their Christmas holidays by feeling anxious and embarrassed, or wondering if they'll be getting fired in the new year!

But, once again, drinking is what happens in the work environment because it's what's always happened.

So that covers the workplace. White-collar or blue, the chances are there's some deeply embedded booze culture to navigate.

Unfortunately, it gets worse. Exposure to alcohol culture often happens long before people get to university, or into the workplace.

My parents went to pubs and clubs, and so did their parents. At school, my friends' parents, like mine, went to pubs and clubs, and so did their parents. It's no surprise - they all live on this planet too!

The result is that we grow up noticing, taking all of it in, and seeing it all as normal. It is normal for many - it's what people do.

Is it a wise or healthy thing to do? No.

Does it make all of those people happy? No.

Does alcohol "suit" everyone? Absolutely not.

But it's often the environment people grow up in, meaning that they reach adulthood not knowing anything different.

Did my parents set out to raise an addict? Of course not. But there were some environmental factors in play that were beyond their control.

I come from an Italian family. Wine is part of Italian culture and has been for generations. My Nonna is 94 years old, and she still can't believe that I can't just have one drink. Not drinking is an alien concept to her, as drinking and "having fun" was a big thing for her generation too.

She actually said to me, at 94 years old, "how do you have fun if you don't drink?!".

I'm not claiming that my Nonna is the problem here! She was brought up within that booze culture, like millions of others. There's also an argument that if she's 94 and still going strong, what's the problem with alcohol?

Well, the answer to that is simple: alcohol doesn't affect everybody in the same way. Some people never have more than one drink at a time! For others, like me, it's like lighting the touchpaper or betting everything on black.

It's not about anybody else, it's about your relationship with alcohol. It's unlikely you'd be reading this if you thought you could "take it or leave it". When alcohol is an emotional crutch, it becomes extremely negative. It's a world away from a glass of wine and the good life it portrays.

It's not just Italians who have alcohol deeply engrained into their national identity. France is known for its wine and champagne, Scotland for its whiskey and Ireland for its Guinness. They're almost the first things you think about when someone mentions their name.

As you can see, my own environment was always very "booze-centric". From childhood, through university, and into the corporate world, alcohol was everywhere.

Alcohol "culture" finds its way into many environments beyond family, education and work. Let's consider the world of sport.

Aside from the athletes who are actually taking part, many of the people on the fringes - the fans and the spectators - tend to drink as part of the experience. Going to the football tends to start with beers and end with more beers. Drunken behaviour often hits the news after large tournaments.

Once again, this is cultural conditioning. If you love your team, what would be wrong with just going to enjoy a game without drinking? Would it be too cynical to suggest that, for many football fans, it's not so much about the love of the game but more about the excuse for boozing every weekend?

The trouble is that most people prefer to follow the crowd than marking themselves out as the "black sheep". Even if, deep down, we don't much like drinking and hate the consequences, it can seem easier just to go along with it.

Over time, we come to see the drunk planet as the normal planet. The issue there is that hangxiety, headaches, empty wallets, depression, vomiting, guilt, shame, and all the other negatives of regular drinking become normal too.

It's not normal. It's completely MENTAL.

You Are Your Environment

However, you also need to be aware of those environmental factors, and how generations of cultural conditioning exist. Without being wise to that, you're vulnerable to being pulled back in. After all, it's all "normal", right?

Take a look at this quote from W Clement Stone, a self-help author, mental health philanthropist, and pioneer of "positive mental attitude":

"You are a product of your environment. So choose the environment that will best develop you toward your objective. Analyse your life in terms of its environment. Are the things around you helping you toward success - or are they holding you back?".

This doesn't mean that you need to quit drinking and then abandon your family, friends, career and favourite sports team! However, it makes a lot of sense to do some serious soul searching.

Ask yourself questions like:

- Is the drinking culture in your workplace holding you back from getting a promotion, pay rise or bonus?

- Are you tolerating your current job because it allows you to "get away" with a work - drink - moan - hangover - work again cycle?

- Are your football mates, your bottomless brunch gang or your clubbing pals causing you to remain in a pattern of overindulgence and regret?

- Do certain friends or family members trigger or encourage you to drink, or fail to support your efforts to do other things?

The answers to questions like that provide you with valuable clues around what you could change about the environments you exist in.

Alcohol is everywhere, but you don't have to say "yes" to it. Back in the third chapter, we talked about the power of saying "no" to friends if you don't fancy certain nights out. The people that matter don't mind, and the people that mind don't matter.

If you wish, you can stay in all of the same environments and do so sober. Giving up drinking doesn't mean changing every aspect of your life, and it's unlikely you'll need to.

However, some particularly boozy environments will inevitably cease to seem so inviting - either because they no longer appeal to you, or because a particular crowd is less accepting of the sober version of you.

That's actually a good thing. It gives you the chance to move into circles of people who fully accept you, and your sobriety. And the thing is, there are many of them. When you're absorbed by booze culture, or hiding hungover from the world, it's easy not to notice them. Furthermore, they don't tend to advertise their existence to heavy drinkers!

I worked in the corporate world for 12 years, but I've never been happier than when I left to become a strength & conditioning coach. Suddenly I was in a world where not drinking is lauded for health reasons, rather than considered "boring" or abnormal.

That simple change of environment turned "normal" on its head.

I swapped pubs and clubs for gyms and bookshops. As a result, my life took a massive leap forward in terms of personal growth. I spend time at golf clubs, at parks, and in coffee shops - with other sober people, and with people who still drink, but respect my life without booze.

There are plenty of sober spaces on this drunk planet. There are sober environments filled with people who share your interests and passions. There are sober spaces populated with people who are more than capable of having fun. There are also plenty of places where non-drinkers mix contentedly with occasional drinkers.

There's a lot of world to explore.

While it does often feel as if much of adult life is centred around booze, there are lots of people who aren't stuck in a constant cycle of drinking.

In 2019, the US National Survey on Drug Use and Health asked adults whether they had drank alcohol in the previous month. 54.9% of them had, but that leaves 45.1% who hadn't. 30.5% hadn't drank in the whole of the past year (NIH, 2022).

That means there's an awful lot of people out there who don't drink at all or only drink occasionally.

Getting your environment right is an important key to being sober on a drunk planet. As this chapter has demonstrated, it's no wonder people follow the herd towards the more obvious places and the culturally embedded ways to have "fun". They've often followed their families, their friends, and their workmates - doing "normal" stuff - sometimes at huge personal cost.

"Normal" doesn't mean "right". And the data actually shows that millions of people enjoy a vastly different "normal".

You can be one of them, and they'll welcome you with open arms.

Chapter 9:

Conclusion

Right at the start of this book, I mentioned how important it is to reframe the idea of "giving up" alcohol. That language implies that you're "giving up" something desirable - that by being sober on a drunk planet, you somehow lose something worth having.

Thanks to alcohol's deeply embedded role in adult life, it's no wonder people fall for that. It's why so many carry on doing something they know to be damaging because they feel like they will "miss out" if they stop.

But life doesn't end when you get sober. Life changes. Life is different. Life is better.

Perhaps if this drunk planet was more of an honest place, it would all be framed rather differently. How about:

- "I'm giving up being overweight".
- "I'm giving up being anxious and depressed".
- "I'm giving up making stupid decisions".
- "I'm giving up my soulless career".
- "I'm giving up headaches and nausea".
- "I'm giving up my toxic relationships".
- "I'm giving up being broke a week after every payday".
- "I'm giving up following what society says is 'fun' and taking ownership of my own happiness".

They're all far more attractive propositions, and far more reflective of what being sober on a drunk planet really involves.

As I said earlier, Sober Sean and Drunk Sean are completely different people. But I didn't get to meet Sober Sean until I quit drinking and began my recovery from alcohol and drugs.

The contrast between who I am now and who I was then is a drastic one. The person who now leaps out of bed ready to meet a personal training client barely recognises the empty, quivering shell who was permanently unwell, overweight, and in debt from buying alcohol and cocaine.

I certainly hit a "rock bottom", but it's not obligatory to do that before you begin your own recovery. In fact, surely it's better if you don't?

If you accept that you're on the wrong path, why wait to travel further down it before taking action? As Einstein said, "insanity is doing the same thing over and over again and expecting different results".

With that in mind, why not try sober life now? I've never met anybody who regrets getting sober, but if you end up being the exception, your old life will still be there waiting for you if that's what you want.

Transforming from "drunk you" to "sober you" isn't an instant thing. Life is different, and there will be a period of adjustment. "Fun" gets redefined. Your new life will likely be filled with different (like-minded) people, different hobbies and activities, and different priorities.

That's perhaps a scary thing, but it's also an incredibly exciting thing. Sober life is more wholesome and filled with nature, gratitude and new experiences.

As Thomas Jefferson once said, "If you want something you've never had, you must be willing to do something you've never done".

If going sober allows you to have all the things you always wanted, then surely it's worth a try?

Since we're talking about giving things up, why don't we reframe it and look at what you give up by NOT giving sober living a try:

- You give up the chance to finally like what you see in the mirror.

- You give up the opportunity to lose weight and build muscle.

- You give up the "sober glow" and the clear skin.

- You give up on a scientifically proven way to improve your mental and physical health.

- You give up a way to drastically reduce your chances of suffering from a host of illnesses - from those that destroy your quality of life, to those that could cut it short.

- You give up on making better decisions.

- You give up on a way to have an enormous amount of extra money to spend.

- You give up on having better relationships with your partner, your friends, your children, and your extended family.

- You give up the chance to date people you have a genuine, sober affinity with.

- You give up on experiencing fulfilling, loving, sober sex.

- You give up on the chance to meet your true "tribe" - the people you have more in common with than a love for the "party" lifestyle.

- You give up on personal growth.

- You give up the opportunity to connect with your spiritual side, and to feed your soul.

- You give up the chance to find out what "fun" can really mean. You swap the genuine, child-like excitement of doing things you love for the repetitive "adult" drudgery of expecting to find fun in a can or a bottle.

- You give up on building a business or career that inspires you daily and stay on the hamster wheel with the majority of other people.

That's a lot of things to give up when the alternative is giving up just one thing - alcohol.

As we reach the end of this book, hopefully, you can see for yourself that sobriety really can "deliver everything alcohol promised". And that giving up alcohol really can be the unexpected shortcut to becoming healthy, happy and financially free.

You may find the following resources helpful:

DrinkAware's alcohol unit and calorie counter: https://www.drinkaware.co.uk/tools/unit-and-calorie-calculator

DrinkAware's Self-Assessment tool to assess your drinking:
https://www.drinkaware.co.uk/tools/self-assessment

The UK NHS guide to alcohol misuse:
https://www.nhs.uk/conditions/alcohol-misuse/

The US CDC's guide to alcohol and public health:
https://www.cdc.gov/alcohol/faqs.htm

A list of alcohol addiction support groups in the USA:
https://www.healthline.com/health/alcohol-addiction-support-groups

Addiction support from the UK NHS:
https://www.nhs.uk/live-well/healthy-body/drug-addiction-getting-help/

Alcohol specific support in the UK:
https://www.nhs.uk/live-well/alcohol-support/

Leave a 1-Click Review!

Customer reviews

5 out of 5

16 global ratings

5 star	100%
4 star	0%
3 star	0%
2 star	0%
1 star	0%

˅ How are ratings calculated?

Review this product

Share your thoughts with other customers

Write a customer review

I would be incredibly thankful if you could just take 60 seconds to write a brief review on Amazon, even if it's just a few sentences.

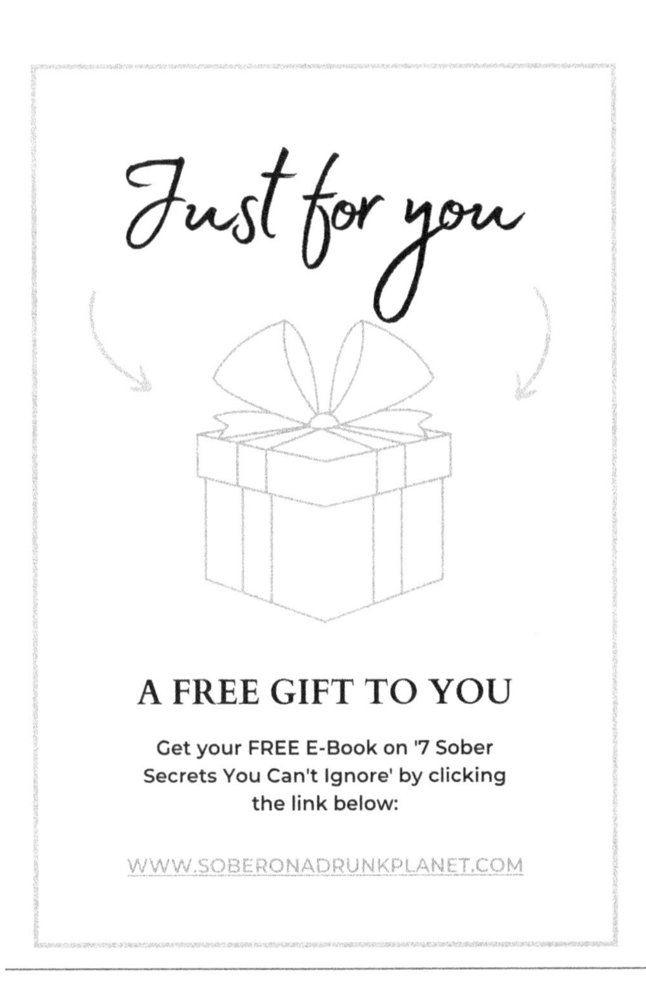
Just for you
A FREE GIFT TO YOU
Get your FREE E-Book on '7 Sober Secrets You Can't Ignore' by clicking the link below:
WWW.SOBERONADRUNKPLANET.COM

Resources and Citations

Introduction

The Guardian. (2018, October 10). Nearly 30% of young people in England do not drink, study finds. Retrieved from https://www.theguardian.com/society/2018/oct/10/young-people-drinking-alcohol-study-england

The Economist. (2019, June 25). What is the most dangerous drug? Retrieved from https://www.economist.com/graphic-detail/2019/06/25/what-is-the-most-dangerous-drug

Chapter 1

NHS UK. What should my daily intake of calories be? Retrieved from https://www.nhs.uk/common-health-questions/food-and-diet/what-should-my-daily-intake-of-calories-be/

Drinkaware. Alcohol and sugar. Retreived from https://www.drinkaware.co.uk/facts/health-effects-of-alcohol/effects-on-the-body/alcohol-and-sugar

Fazzino, T.L, Fleming, K, Sher, K, Sullivan, D, Befort, C. (2017). Heavy Drinking in Young Adulthood Increases Risk of Transitioning to Obesity. PMC Journal, 53(2), 169-175. Retrieved from https://www.ncbi.nlm.nih.gov/pmc/articles/PMC5522652/

Drinkaware. Calories in alcohol. Retrieved from https://www.drinkaware.co.uk/facts/health-effects-of-alcohol/alcohol-and-calories/calories-in-alcohol

NHS UK. Calories in alcohol. Retrieved from https://www.nhs.uk/live-well/alcohol-support/calories-in-alcohol/

Drinkaware. Unit and calorie counter. Retrieved from https://www.drinkaware.co.uk/tools/unit-and-calorie-calculator

Tremblay, A, St-Pierre, S. (1996, April 1). The hyperphagic effect of a high-fat diet and alcohol intake persists after control for energy density. Retrieved from https://academic.oup.com/ajcn/article/63/4/479/4651176

McDonald's. Big Mac Combo Meal. Retrieved from https://www.mcdonalds.com/us/en-us/meal/big-mac-meal.html

Parr, E, Carmera, D, Areta, J, Burke, L, Philips, S, Hawley, J, Coffey, V. (2014). Alcohol Ingestion Impairs Maximal Post-Exercise Rates of Myofibrillar Protein Synthesis following a Single Bout of Concurrent Training. Plos One, 10.1371. Retrieved from https://journals.plos.org/plosone/article?id=10.1371/journal.pone.0088384

Wasylenko, J. 10 Reasons Why Exercise Makes You Happier. Retrieved from https://www.lifehack.org/articles/lifestyle/10-reasons-why-exercise-makes-you-happier.html

Silver Maple Recovery. Why You Crave Sweets When You Stop Drinking. Retrieved from https://www.silvermaplerecovery.com/blog/sugar-cravings-after-quitting-alcohol/

WebMD (2020, April 14). How Drinking Alcohol Affects Your Skin. Retrieved from https://www.webmd.com/mental-health/addiction/ss/slideshow-alcohol-skin

Pan, J., Cen, L., Chen, W., Yu, C., Li, Y., & Shen, Z. (2019). Alcohol Consumption and the Risk of Gastroesophageal Reflux Disease: A Systematic Review and Meta-analysis. Alcohol and alcoholism (Oxford, Oxfordshire), 54(1), 62–69. https://doi.org/10.1093/alcalc/agy063

NHS UK. Heart Burn and Acid Reflux. Retrieved from https://www.nhs.uk/conditions/heartburn-and-acid-reflux/

Libbert, L (2021, June 11). What alcohol can do to your midlife gut health. Retrieved from https://www.telegraph.co.uk/health-fitness/body/glass-red-wine-can-good-gut-stick-one/

Recovery Nutrition (2021, June 25). How to age well - the gut / inflammation link. Retrieved from https://www.recovery-nutrition.co.uk/blog/how-to-age-well-the-gut-chronic-inflammation-link

Mind And Body Works. The Gut-Brain Connection: The relationship to emotions and managing stress. Retrieved from https://mindandbodyworks.com/the-gut-brain-connection-the-relationship-to-emotions-and-managing-stress/

World Health Organization (2018, September 21). Harmful use of alcohol kills more than 3 million people each year, most of them men. Retrieved from https://www.who.int/news/item/21-09-2018-harmful-use-of-alcohol-kills-more-than-3-million-people-each-year--most-of-them-men

Drinkaware. Alcohol Withdrawal. Retrieved from https://www.drinkaware.co.uk/facts/health-effects-of-alcohol/mental-health/alcohol-withdrawal-symptoms

CDC. Alcohol Use and Your Health. Retrieved from https://www.cdc.gov/alcohol/fact-sheets/alcohol-use.htm

Therrien, A (2018, April 13). Regular excess drinking can take years off your life, study finds. Retrieved from https://www.bbc.co.uk/news/health-43738644

Healthline. Is Alcohol a Stimulant? Retrieved from https://www.healthline.com/nutrition/is-alcohol-a-stimulant

AddictionCenter. Is Alcohol A Depressant? https://www.addictioncenter.com/alcohol/is-alcohol-a-depressant/

Buddy T (2020, October 1). Chronic Drinking Increases Cortisol Levels. Retrieved from https://www.verywellmind.com/heavy-drinking-increases-stress-hormone-63201#

Loria, K (2017, January 1). Everything we know about hangovers — and what you can do to make the pain go away. Retrieved from https://www.businessinsider.com/how-to-fix-cure-deal-with-a-hangover-2016-12?r=US&IR=T

WebMD (2020, December 13). What Is Cortisol? Retrieved from https://www.webmd.com/a-to-z-guides/what-is-cortisol

Hayes, A (2018, August 29). How stress sabotages muscle building and weightloss goals. Retrieved from https://www.menshealth.com/uk/health/a759406/how-stress-sabotages-muscle-building-and-weight-loss-goals/

DeNoon, D (2006, August 28). Fog of Alcoholism Clears With Sobriety. Retrieved from https://www.webmd.com/mental-health/addiction/news/20060828/fog-alcoholism-clears-sobriety

Masterson, L (2022, February 10). Drunk Driving Statistics 2022. Retrieved from https://www.forbes.com/advisor/car-insurance/drunk-driving-statistics/

Chapter 2

Calic, N (2022, January 27). Debt Statistics UK Edition [2022]. Retrieved from https://cybercrew.uk/blog/debt-statistics-uk/

The Calculator Site. Compound Interest Calculator. Retrieved from https://www.thecalculatorsite.com/finance/calculators/compoundinterestcalculator.php

Chapter 3

NHS. Alcohol Misuse - Risks. Retrieved from https://www.nhs.uk/conditions/alcohol-misuse/risks/

Iliades, C (2012, January 4). Why Boozing Can Be Bad for Your Sex Life. Retrieved from https://www.everydayhealth.com/erectile-dysfunction/why-boozing-can-be-bad-for-your-sex-life.aspx

Healthline. Why Am I Dry Down There All of A Sudden? Retrieved from https://www.healthline.com/health/why-am-i-dry-down-there-all-of-a-sudden

Drinkaware. Is alcohol harming your fertility? Retrieved from https://www.drinkaware.co.uk/facts/health-effects-of-alcohol/alcohol-fertility-and-pregnancy/is-alcohol-harming-your-fertility

MentalHelp.net. What Happens to Children of Alcoholic Parents? Retrieved from https://www.mentalhelp.net/parenting/what-happens-to-children-of-alcoholic-parents/

Chapter 5

Oxford Languages. Spirituality Dictionary Definition. Retrieved from https://www.google.com/search?q=spirituality+dictionary+definition

Alcoholics Anonymous. Frequently Asked Questions. Retrieved from https://www.alcoholics-anonymous.org.uk/professionals/frequently-asked-questions

American Osteopathic Association. The Benefits of Yoga. Retrieved from https://osteopathic.org/what-is-osteopathic-medicine/benefits-of-yoga/

The Good Body (2022, January 14). 41 Yoga Statistics: Discover Its (Ever-increasing) Popularity. Retrieved from https://www.thegoodbody.com/yoga-statistics/

FinancesOnline. 50 Essential Meditation Statistics for 2022: Benefits, Technology & Practice Data. Retrieved from https://financesonline.com/meditation-statistics/

The Good Body (2022, January 13). 27 Meditation Statistics: Data and Trends Revealed for 2022. Retrieved from https://www.thegoodbody.com/meditation-statistics

Chapter 6

IWSR. No- and Low-Alcohol in Key Global Markets Reaches Almost US$10 Billion in Value. Retrieved from https://www.theiwsr.com/no-and-low-alcohol-in-key-global-markets-reaches-almost-us10-billion-in-value/

Chapter 7

Clifton, J (2017, June 13). The World's Broken Workplace. Retrieved from https://news.gallup.com/opinion/chairman/212045/world-broken-workplace.aspx

Renewal Lodge (2019, August 14). 5 Ways Quitting Drinking Affects Your Brain. Retrieved from https://www.renewallodge.com/5-ways-quitting-drinking-affects-your-brain/

Gov.UK (2021, November 29). Self-employment. Retrieved from https://www.ethnicity-facts-figures.service.gov.uk/work-pay-and-benefits/employment/self-employment/

Vista (2018, January 15). Expectations vs. reality: what's it really like to go it alone?. Retrieved from https://news.vistaprint.com/expectations-vs-reality

Chapter 8

Roberts, J (2018, December 5). One in 10 people fired or disciplined for Christmas party mayhem. Retrieved from https://metro.co.uk/2018/12/05/one-10-people-fired-disciplined-christmas-party-mayhem-8210628/

NIH National Institute on Alcohol Abuse and Alcoholism (2022, March). Alcohol Facts and Statistics. Retrieved from https://www.niaaa.nih.gov/publications/brochures-and-fact-sheets/alcohol-facts-and-statistics

Sober On A Drunk Planet:

3 SOBER STEPS

An Uncommon Guide To Stop Drinking
and Master Your Sobriety

By Sean Alexander

"When we are no longer able to change a situation – we are challenged to change ourselves."

- Viktor Frankl.

Introduction – 3 Sober Steps

How many times have you said, "never again!" – after a big weekend, a night "on the sesh", or just another evening when you gave in and popped the cork on a second bottle of wine?

If the answer is a scarily high number, you're not alone. Research suggests that the average person endures nearly 2,000 hangovers in their lifetime[1]. That equates to spending over five YEARS suffering. And for regular drinkers, the numbers are likely even higher.

At that moment, when you wake up with a banging head, a churning stomach, a horrific taste in your mouth and a crippling feeling of anxiety, you *do mean it* when you say, "never again".

But somehow you end up back there – you wake up with a jolt, the previous evening flashes before your eyes, and the living nightmare repeats itself. So you add to your ever-growing list of "never agains", perhaps adding, "I *mean* it this time!"

Perhaps you are sick and tired of feeling sick and tired or have one of many other reasons to at least try a life that doesn't involve hangovers, poor decisions and regret.

Luckily, you are here. It shows you want to learn how to stop drinking alcohol and put the action in to stay sober. And that's a powerful place to start.

But don't be fooled.

Knowing you should quit drinking and 'doing the work' to stop drinking are very different things. It's like knowing that alcohol makes you miserable but never doing anything about it!

The problem is that our brains are hardwired to do the easy things we have always done (drinking!), and anything that challenges the norm is seen as a threat.

That threat manifests itself as lies, manipulation and "f*ck it" moments to make us believe we can have "one drink".

And when was the last time you just had one drink?

Knowing you should stop drinking but not being able to stop can be really damaging to all areas of your life. It often leads to a destructive cycle of self-sabotage that feeds a negative feedback loop of drink > hangover > regret > repeat.

Everyone has their reasons for stopping drinking and wanting to stay sober. They are all valid. Sometimes, many things can happen, and we *still* don't change our drinking habits.

Quitting alcohol will directly challenge everything you think you know. But giving up alcohol goes far beyond just changing how you think. It involves changing how you move, how you eat and how you live day to day.

Old ways won't open new doors.

3 Sober Steps will show you powerful new ways to open exciting new doors that will help you quit drinking and stay sober – if that's what you want. The *3 Sober Steps* will radically transform how you approach your sobriety and allow you to make healthier choices on auto-pilot.

Those healthier choices directly feed into a positive feedback loop that keeps you in a cycle of doing good things with better outcomes, not destructive things with negative outcomes.

Throughout this book, we will reaffirm the *3 Sober Steps*: **Self-Awareness, Positive Action** and **Intuition**.

Let's explore them in more detail below:

1. Creating Self-Awareness

Without building self-awareness around how alcohol was negatively impacting your life, you wouldn't be here now. You would still be blind to the fact that alcohol was the cause of most (if not all) of your problems, and you would still be drinking. That's a dangerous place to be.

Building self-awareness allows you to discover *why* you keep drinking the way you do – and it's the initial foundation to help you stop drinking alcohol and stay sober.

Habits form for all kinds of different reasons. Unravelling why you do what you do requires the type of self-reflection many people shy away from, but it comes with massive rewards.

The reality is that we all make many of our decisions subconsciously – often using mechanisms that developed in childhood. Past events and trauma may have moulded your behaviour in ways you've not even considered.

You will have built a lifestyle around alcohol that has been repeated so many times it created its own auto-pilot. Before you know it, you are three drinks in, and the cycle of hangover > regret > repeat starts again. Building self-awareness is about stopping auto-pilot from happening and giving you back control.

This book will give you the tools to take your self-awareness to a whole new level. It will educate you on the importance of the subconscious mind, neuroplasticity and how powerful our thoughts can be for creating our reality.

But having the knowledge to change is pretty useless if you don't use it.

2. Taking Positive Action

It's easy to *say* you're going to do something. You could *say* – right now – that you're going to run a marathon, qualify as a doctor, or launch the next household-name tech start-up.

But the people who do those things must put in the physical training, complete the years of university study, or withstand the highs, lows, and knock-backs of the business world.

Giving up drinking is no different.

It all comes down to taking action and staying sober means *continuing* to take action. Aside from working on self-awareness, there's the need to make the right choices and do the work consistently. "Doing the work" ranges from having the courage to self-reflect and ask yourself challenging questions to having the confidence to follow your own path – rather than following the herd to the bar every Friday night.

The good news is that this all gets much easier over time. As you will discover shortly, the mind is capable of profound change. In time, you can begin to take healthy and rewarding actions subconsciously instead of doing the destructive behaviours you've always done – on auto-pilot.

As we go through the chapters, you will read about incredibly powerful tools, from understanding how to regulate emotions to proven tools to combat triggers that require you to take action. These tools will not only help you to quit drinking, but they will also assist you in every area of your life.

At the end of each chapter, there will be a short task to help you practice taking action whilst challenging your subconscious beliefs and raising your self-awareness.

Based on the notion that action is power, you will see that I refer to *taking positive action* throughout the book. Not all actions are equal, and just like drinking alcohol and taking drugs, not all actions are positive!

Remember: If an action doesn't move you towards your end goal - to stop drinking alcohol and stay sober - then it's NOT a positive action.

3. Building Your Intuition

Over time, working on your self-awareness and taking consistent action allows you to build a finely tuned sense of intuition. This creates a positive feedback loop where you subconsciously *know* the right things to do for your mind, body and soul.

You will learn how intuition is key to replacing the negative feedback loop of drink > hangover > regret > repeat with a positive feedback loop that can run on a new auto-pilot.

Getting drunk every weekend and enduring hangovers every week is a feedback loop too – but it's not one you want in your life. It's the exact feedback loop that results in all of those "never agains".

***

So who is this book for?

If you are serious about quitting alcohol and using tools that will help you live a life you can be proud of – this book is for you.

Even if you have been sober for some time, the tools in this book will increase your resilience and help elevate every area of your life. You will finish the book feeling like a sober Jedi, ready to master being sober on a drunk planet.

It is crucial, at this point, to mention that quitting alcohol "cold turkey" can be extremely dangerous for regular and heavy drinkers due to physical withdrawal symptoms. These can include nausea, insomnia, shaky hands and headaches, and life-threatening things such as seizures, hallucinations and hypertension.[2] Therefore, you must contact your doctor before abstaining from alcohol if you have even the slightest suspicion that you may be physically dependent.

The resources section at the back of this book provides more material about physical withdrawals. By reading these, you will become more *self-aware* and be able to take *positive action* for your specific needs

Don't leave it to chance – if you think you might be suffering from alcohol withdrawals – speak to a medical professional now. This is your call to *action.*

***

This book is a follow-up to *Sober on a Drunk Planet – Giving Up Alcohol.* However, it is intentionally designed to work as a complementary read *or* as a standalone work. The previous book makes you question why alcohol was ever part of your life in the first place and provides you with *leverage* towards becoming sober. This book takes the next step in that journey - giving you the processes and tools to stop drinking alcohol and stay sober.

The guidance in this book is drawn from years of "eureka moments" from getting sober, which included attending rehab, Anonymous groups, group therapy, and LOTS of individual therapy. Having become obsessed with self-development in sobriety, I have spent over 3000 hours listening to and reading books on the subject.

As a qualified therapist and strength coach, I also take inspiration from my professional experience helping people build stronger bodies and minds. Further pearls of wisdom have been picked up from the Sober On A Drunk Planet Community and the many people I've interviewed on the Sober On A Drunk Planet podcast.

I spent many years being self-aware enough to know I *should* give up drinking. Any "pleasure" it gave me was far outweighed by the destruction it was having on everything from my finances to my physical and mental health. But there's a clear difference between knowing you *should* do something and taking positive action.

Sobriety creates a life-changing positive feedback loop that rewards you again and again. It replaces the *negative* feedback loop of get drunk > throw away your leisure time being hungover > go to work miserable > do it all again next week because that's what you've always done.

You NEVER have to do that again.

Before we begin, here's a quick synopsis of what you can expect in the coming pages:

In the first chapter, we start that all-important work on self-awareness. First, we look at how much of what we do is based on subconscious decisions and how that keeps so many people in a negative feedback loop of "never agains".

You already know that drinking week after week and building up an ever-growing mass of regret and poor self-esteem is doing you no good. While you read the first chapter, you will begin to understand why you do it – and how to *stop* doing it.

Chapter Two focuses on the importance of setting goals, teaching you how to evolve from somebody who talks about your plans to somebody who actually takes action. It also discusses the importance of intuition and why developing it is the 'secret sauce' to mastering your sobriety.

Chapter Three focuses on emotional intelligence and how drinking regularly is a guaranteed way to compromise it. It teaches you how to regulate your emotions healthily rather than dull them with alcohol. This chapter is vital for sustained sobriety and eliminating the big red "f*ck it" button that has haunted all of us!

Chapter Four focuses on cravings and triggers and how to recognise and combat them. Cravings and triggers are why many people find staying sober much more difficult than initially quitting drinking. Once you understand how they work and learn the life-changing tools in this book, you'll have the power to resist them.

In Chapter Five, you'll learn about the ego. Understanding it can be the key to long-lasting, contented sobriety. You'll also meet "Tommy Tequila" and "Wendy the wino" and find out how you can evolve from having a drunken ego to managing a positive sober ego.

Chapter Six is all about strengthening your sobriety and making it last. It's about building resilience and positive habits.

As habits go, regular drinking requires determination and commitment. “Living life on hard mode” is an expression you often hear to describe what it takes to wade through life with hangovers and low energy levels – let alone poor physical health and an overdraft!

Positive habits are infinitely more rewarding. This chapter helps you start building positive habits that lead to healthier feedback loops.

Chapter Seven discusses the link between mind and body. Despite the number of questionable articles about how the occasional glass of wine is “good for you,” none of them cancel out the reality that alcohol IS a poison that is seriously detrimental to both physical and mental health.

Understanding the importance of exercise and nutrition is key to living a healthy and rewarding life without alcohol. We explore the science behind this so you can make decisions that genuinely make you feel good.

Finally, Chapter Eight talks about energy and both positive and negative vibrations. Millions of people worldwide engage in practices focusing on energy flow – from acupuncture to reiki and Qigong.

Whether or not those activities appeal to you (at this stage) isn't something to worry about. You needn't be a Qigong fanatic to feel different energies around you – from people, environments, and situations. The energy you feel at the end of a Sunday morning gym session is very different to the energy you feel the morning after a heavy night on the booze!

Once again, self-awareness plays a big part here. Awareness of your own energy and the energy around you helps ensure that your sobriety isn't derailed by the places you go, the things you do, and the people you choose to spend time with.

Throughout all the chapters, we continually return to the key theme of the *3 Sober Steps*:

Enhanced **self-awareness**, combined with **positive action**, will allow you to develop your

intuition – enabling you to make better, healthier, and more rewarding decisions.

If it doesn't challenge you, it doesn't change you - *3 Sober Steps* will constantly challenge you to *know* more, *do* more and *feel* more so you can stop drinking and master your sobriety.

Are you ready to turn "never again!" into "let's do THAT again!?" Let's start and begin to work on the rewarding art of self-awareness.

Chapter 1:

You Don't Know What You Don't Know (And What You DO Know Might Not Be Correct!)

What IS self-awareness?

The dictionary definition is "knowledge and understanding of your own character".[3] However, in 1972, two psychologists put forward a rather more informative description:

"Self-awareness is the ability to focus on yourself and how your actions, thoughts, or emotions do or don't align with your internal standards. If you're highly self-aware, you can objectively evaluate yourself, manage your emotions, align your behaviour with your values, and understand correctly how others perceive you."[4]

Let's apply that to drinking alcohol regularly, and think back to the hungover, "never again" feeling we talked about in the introduction.

If you're regularly regretting your behaviour, it's certainly not aligning with your values. And if, yet again, you've woken up having consumed more alcohol than you intended to, your actions haven't aligned with your internal standards either!

The good news is that you're far from alone. Self-awareness is a skill that plenty of people struggle to develop. Think about your friends and family. No doubt you can readily think of how certain people have patterns of behaviour that are clear to everyone but themselves. It's perhaps even obvious what changes they should make.

It's harder to turn the lens on yourself. The rewards are huge, but it takes courage to do it. And it's certainly not something you can do whilst caught in a cycle of being drunk and being hungover.

So how does being more self-aware help you to give up drinking and stay sober?

To help you make the connection, here's another quote associated with the inspiring Austrian psychiatrist and philosopher Viktor Frankl.[5]

"Between stimulus and response, there is a space. In that space lies our freedom and power to choose our response. In our response lies our growth and freedom."

Millions of people respond to all kinds of stimulus by drinking alcohol. Tough week at work? Straight to the bar for happy hour – for yet another "just one or two" that turns into an all-nighter. Something to celebrate? Bottle of Champagne. Sun's come out? Better get the beers in! Your team won? Drink to celebrate. Your team lost? Drink to commiserate.

It might seem it's what *everybody* does. In your social circle, it may *be* what everybody does! But it's NOT everybody. A study of the world's adult population showed that 58% of people hadn't consumed any alcohol at all in the previous 12 months.[6]

Those people get bad news too. They have tough weeks at work, attend weddings and funerals, and deal with all of the good and bad things that life throws at them. (And they don't have to do any of it with a hangover!)

It seems insane that drinking alcohol appears to be the automatic response to so many different things, both good and bad. It IS insane, but it's not quite as simple as that.

When you close down your email after a gruelling week, you don't consciously sit there and think, "what is the best solution to my feelings of tiredness, powerlessness and frustration?" Instead, we all make many decisions subconsciously based on what those around us do, how we've been conditioned, and what we think will get us through the day.

Alcohol *does* relieve stress (in an extremely limited and temporary way). Alcohol *does* "make us forget". But do you truly believe that it's the solution to stress? If you spend all weekend drinking, do you feel less stressed when you roll nauseously back into work on Monday morning? Do you feel proud that you spent more than you'd intended and achieved none of the productive things you planned to?

The thing is, we are conditioned to see alcohol as a solution. TV adverts show people looking glamorous and carefree while they drink 40% spirits. They never show the morning after, because let's face it, you would never buy it again if they advertised all the adverse effects that came with it! We're surrounded by "wine o'clock" culture, bars, restaurants, and shops selling booze.

When you become aware of what alcohol actually does to you versus what society has been conditioning you to believe – you start to shift your focus.

Why What We Believe May Not Be True

For years of drinking, I went around with the flawed beliefs that alcohol was a positive influence on my life:

- I believed that alcohol was the only way to celebrate downtime and socialise.
- I believed alcohol was the cure to a stressful week and an effective way to deal with my problems.
- I believed that alcohol made me more attractive to the opposite sex.
- I believed I was funnier when I was drunk, and people told me that too (which confirmed my belief)!
- I believed not drinking alcohol made me less of a man.
- I believed that people who didn't drink couldn't be trusted.
- I believed I was a better driver when I had a drink (illegal and dangerous).

These beliefs were created through a combination of:

- Societal conditioning (I live in London, and yes, us Brits have rightly earned our reputation for boozing!)
- Family and cultural conditioning (I am half Irish and half Italian – Guinness *and* wine!)
- Growing up with friends who were subjected to EXACTLY the same set of beliefs around alcohol.

These beliefs around alcohol were reaffirmed at school, University, the corporate world, my golf club, football club, rugby club, cricket club and even the one time I went to a running club (never again!). Alcohol was always a HUGE part of these places.

Even every occasion I went to reaffirmed those beliefs. Holidays, birthdays, funerals, weddings, divorce parties, business networking, festivals, dating, easter, picnics, river cruises, star gazing, sunrises, sunsets, Christmas, new years eve, new years day, and the list goes on.

Even one of the most popular groups on Peloton is #pelo4wine. Sweating your proverbial balls off for an hour to reward yourself with a chemical depressant seems crazy. But, even with fitness, we have groups of people that reaffirm the message – alcohol is the reward!

We really do live on a drunk planet.

When you are around people who all believe the same things, you never do anything differently that might upset the "norm". Going teetotal at any stage before rehab went against everything I believed!

As you can see, all the conditioning acts to do is create a set of beliefs about alcohol. Those beliefs are then re-affirmed by the people you hang out with in the places you visit or even the Peloton group you join!

You have no chance of changing until you open yourself up to the possibility that **what you believe, might not be true**. These are called flawed beliefs.

My flawed belief - that drinking alcohol made me more attractive and confident with women – went directly against the reality. I was hopelessly single for most of my twenties! And there were far more embarrassing stories than there were romantic ones. So, was my belief that alcohol made me more attractive and confident correct?

No. It really wasn't!

Here's another example of a flawed belief:

"I needed that" are words often spoken by those who believe alcohol can relieve stress. Yes, we have all been there!

If we think alcohol will relieve stress, it's no wonder we head to the bar after a stressful week or open a bottle of wine at home. But the problem becomes apparent when we realise that feeding alcohol to an already stressed body and brain is the worst possible thing we could do.

In my previous book, *Sober on a Drunk Planet - Giving Up Alcohol,* I delved into the science of this. In order to process alcohol, the body releases cortisol. Cortisol is literally known as "the stress hormone".[7] It's a physiological impossibility for alcohol to truly relieve stress.

To deal with this paradox, we engage in something known as cognitive dissonance. This is "the mental conflict that occurs when a person's behaviours and beliefs do not align".[8]

Why We Do What We Do, When We Really Know We Shouldn't

Cognitive dissonance can creep into all kinds of areas of your life. The theory goes that people feel "unease and tension" when they hold "two beliefs that contradict one another". It's like wanting to be fit and healthy but never going to the gym. You feel guilty as a result of not going to the gym and upset at not being fit and healthy!

In order to feel more comfortable, people indulge in various behaviours to relieve the discomfort. For example, they may "explain things away" or "reject information that conflicts with their existing beliefs".

Maintaining cognitive dissonance is an *easier* and more comfortable option than doing what you *should* be doing – especially if it involves challenging beliefs that may have been embedded since childhood.

It's no different with drinking alcohol. For example, when you hear someone say, "I don't drink as much as so and so", all they are doing is explaining away the notion that they might be problematic drinkers themselves. I used to deflect my drinking and drugging on everyone and anything - to avoid having to sit with the reality of what was actually happening.

Cognitive dissonance is most noticeable when a drinker has been told by a doctor that the recommended maximum amount is six beers or six glasses of wine per week.[9] We seem to forget that when we are eight drinks down on a Friday night!

Once you know the risks and realities of drinking (and it's not hard to learn them), you *have* to engage in cognitive dissonance to keep doing it. Likewise, once you know the science and realise that alcohol doesn't relieve stress, you *need* cognitive dissonance to keep telling yourself it does.

The mental gymnastics required to keep this up are exhausting, but people do it for decades. I did. Some people keep it up for a lifetime.

There are various ways to maintain cognitive dissonance.[10] You'll no doubt recognise them - in yourself and the people around you.

One is "refusing to absorb new information that goes against (your) ideas". This means paying attention to those questionable "red wine is good for you" articles - but ignoring the many others that speak of very real health risks.

This is a phenomenon known as “priming”[11], where your brain selectively filters out information that conflicts with your existing beliefs – or what you *want* to believe - in order to continue your life without having to make any challenging changes.

For example: “Alcohol makes me attractive to women” versus “I need to get sober and work on self-esteem issues that I've had since I was child - so I can one day attract someone with my natural charm!”

The brain is already exhausted at contemplating option two, so it defaults to what's easiest – next pint please!

Another way people maintain cognitive dissonance is “excluding themselves from participating in discussions about specific topics”. For drinkers, an easy way to do that is to stick with the same regular drinking crowd. It feels normal when everyone is doing it.

When someone introduces themselves as sober to one of these drinking groups, you will hear people make justifications about their drinking and how they "don't drink that often"! The drinkers feel that they need to defend themselves!

Famous economist John Kenneth Galbraith said, "faced with the choice between changing one's mind and proving that there is no need to do so, almost everyone opts for the latter"[12]. That's cognitive dissonance right there.

The alternative to cognitive dissonance is to challenge and change your beliefs.

This means being ready to evolve – and that *is* more challenging than simply doing the same thing over and over again. It means daring to read the scary articles (and perhaps your bank statements)! It means choosing which of those conflicting beliefs and behaviours you truly wish to spend the rest of your days living by. And if you're stuck in the "never again" cycle, it might already be clear which beliefs aren't working for you.

We will look at ways you can improve your self-awareness and challenge those flawed beliefs shortly.

Self-Awareness And The Inner Child

Challenging and changing your beliefs also means getting in touch with your inner child and becoming more *self-aware* about how your early experiences moulded you.

Why is this important to stop drinking and stay sober?

It's rarely the alcohol or the drugs that are the underlying problem. Instead, addiction becomes a secondary problem to covering up past events or trauma.

It's because many of the thought patterns that feed your emotions (and, in turn, your actions) began to form long before you were aware of it. Studies have even suggested that "there are significant links between our behavioural tendencies when we're just a few months old and our later personality".[13]

This doesn't mean that you were born as somebody who was always going to drink too much. However, it's hard to argue with the fact that our early experiences impact how we see ourselves and interact with the world around us. To paraphrase a quote from scientist Dr Carl Sagan[14], "until we fully understand our past, we may never truly live in the present".

Trauma is a tricky subject. It means different things to different people. It's all relative, and there's no threshold at which childhood trauma should be considered bad enough to impact your adult life.

Clearly, some varieties of childhood trauma have obvious implications. For example, children subjected to physical, sexual or emotional abuse are likely to experience distressing triggers in adulthood, often leading to abuse of alcohol and other substances. Numerous studies prove this link.[15] But trauma comes in all shapes and sizes.

Many people go through their adult lives convinced they didn't experience any notable childhood trauma. They don't consider that feeling excluded in the playground because they weren't sporty, or didn't have the same toys as their peers, could have been seriously traumatic for their inner child. It could well have created coping mechanisms that remain to this day.

There's an endless number of similar examples: growing up in the shadow of a gifted sibling, being ignored or neglected, feeling different, or living in a household that was coping with health, financial or any one of thousands of other issues.

Often, the reaction to this trauma and the compulsion to "bury it" happens in the subconscious. As a result, you may not even remember childhood events that played a massive part in making you who you are.

That's why self-awareness and getting in touch with that inner child is so important. It gets you to that point where you don't only know what you do but also *why you do it*.

Focusing on the solution only, i.e. stopping drinking alcohol, is only part of the equation for a strong recovery. Overcoming past trauma by reliving it in the present is how we become stronger and more resilient to traumatic responses.

If an event triggers you, it can be incredibly overpowering and lead you to reach for the bottle for temporary relief. The event could be someone speaking to you in a certain way or touching a part of your body that puts you back into a moment of past trauma. All of this can happen subconsciously without you having any conscious control.

Doing the inner child work is a HUGE part of managing future situations. It will help you move past and manage those past traumas so they no longer impact you today.

It IS possible to wrestle back control of your subconscious using a process known as subconscious rewiring (or reprogramming). As you become more self-aware, you can slow things down and stop that cycle from happening on auto-pilot.

Subconscious rewiring begins "with deciding what you want – right now and in the future – and focusing on it".[16] As you work through this book, you will become more self-aware and start to understand and challenge some of your subconscious beliefs.

Developing Self-Awareness For Sobriety And Beyond

As we've established, self-awareness holds the key to shaking ourselves out of old patterns and developing healthier behaviours. Thankfully, there are *many* ways to work on it.

Some of the ideas below will probably appeal to you more than others. While it may prove tempting to gravitate to those, perhaps consider a quote from American philosopher Ralph Waldo Emerson: "always do what you are afraid to do".[17]

The strategies you dismiss may well be those that would benefit you most. If, for example, you're convinced that you wouldn't benefit from therapy, ask yourself if you're "explaining things away" or "rejecting information that conflicts with your existing beliefs". If so, it might be worth flicking back to the section on cognitive dissonance earlier in this chapter!

Here are critical ways to raise your self-awareness around alcohol so you can arm yourself with a vital ingredient for change – knowledge.

Learning and Gaining New Knowledge

Neuroscience has shown that when we learn new things, the brain creates new neural pathways and can "alter existing ones".[18] This ability to continually change the makeup of the brain is known as neuroplasticity.

When I was in rehab, they told us to buy new clothes, drive home different ways and move furniture around in our bedrooms. The goal was to stimulate our neuroplasticity and distract our addictive minds from the many things we associated with drugs and alcohol. By the time I went to rehab, *everything* was a reminder of drugs and alcohol!

It was great advice. Even a drive past my local pub was enough to set a chain of events that would see me arriving home five days later! When I started to change things up, my mind started losing those associations (more on that later) and my urges to drink and use drugs weakened over time.

It's never too late for your brain to evolve and your subconscious to start making healthier decisions. You don't reach adulthood with a fully developed brain. In fact, the brain never stops changing in response to learning.

Books, blog articles, audiobooks, online courses, group therapy, biographies...all of those things contain knowledge that can increase your self-awareness. Often, it's not about agreeing with every word you read or listen to but finding just one or two "knowledge bombs" that resonate with you or make you question your long-held beliefs.

You could read a memoir of a sports or musical hero and hear how *their* childhood impacted their adult decisions. It may cause you to have a new realisation about your own past. You could listen to an absorbing podcast that you find interesting and relatable. You could read "quit lit" books and tales of addiction - and find out what other people have learned about themselves when quitting alcohol and other drugs.

You may not be a natural reader. Some people prefer auditory or visual learning. Thankfully, we live in a world with easy access to podcasts, Audible books and videos on demand. So there are plenty of ways to absorb knowledge, get those new neural pathways firing, and take in information that could make us more self-aware.

Whether you prefer to read the words or listen to them, the fact remains that for a region of about £15($18) or less, you can absorb the fruits of somebody's entire career and all of their valuable insights. Having worked as a Financial Advisor, I can safely say that the best return on investment you will ever get is from reading and listening to books!

You can often learn something new from reading something old. You can read about the experiences of people who've overcome similar problems to your own. You can enjoy finding out how your own personal heroes have learned to thrive.

Here's a tip: Find a subject you're interested in and read (or listen) to three books from the most well-known authors in that field. This will give you the best insights into any topic - for a fraction of the price, time and energy involved in becoming a professor in that topic. So if you want to quit alcohol for good – get reading and listening to those books that will guide you to stop drinking alcohol.

Don't underestimate the life-changing impact that learning new things can have on your self-awareness, especially if it's something you've not done in a while. Education makes us more robust and more resilient to potential relapses.

Seeking Feedback

Feedback is one of the best tools we have to understand how people perceive us, our behaviour and our work.

There's nothing to stop you from directly seeking this feedback – from your friends, family, bosses and colleagues.

Of course, many people avoid seeking such feedback – due to the fear of having their egos dented by hearing something negative. This fear can cause them to avoid asking for feedback or ignore it to protect their ego.

We will learn about managing the ego later in the book. But, for now, it's sufficient to say that becoming "teachable" and receptive to feedback is one of the best things you can do to boost your self-awareness.

Consider the alternative: Refusing to listen, refusing to grow, and remaining stuck in the same cycle.

We can all learn from others – people with relevant experience and expertise (yes, that applies to people who are younger than us!).

There's absolutely no reason to think that your boss would be anything other than pleased to be asked what you could do to improve your performance at work. Likewise, there's no reason your partner wouldn't be willing to tell you three things you could do to improve your relationship or make their life easier! Giving up alcohol might be one of them!

Becoming "teachable" in this way takes guts, but it's a fantastic way to become more self-aware and begin to unlearn destructive behaviours and work on new and better ones.

Being receptive to feedback is a path to growth and long-term sobriety.

Reflecting on Your Actions and Asking Powerful Questions

A great way to open up those new neural pathways is to have the grit to ask yourself powerful and searching questions.

When we drink regularly, we tend to drink with other drinkers – people we may convince ourselves are like-minded people. The fact that the main thing we may have in common with those people is a fondness for alcohol is for a whole separate discussion (one you will find in *Sober on a Drunk Planet - Giving Up Alcohol*).

The reality is that when you're with those like-minded people, you don't tend to ask yourselves the powerful questions that matter. Questions like:

"Where am I going in my life?"

"Why did I reach for that bottle last night?"

"What's really going on for me?"

"Are hangovers really a sign of a 'good night' out?

It can prove challenging and painful to ask those questions and consider the answers.

It's way easier to have another drink.

The thing is, it's the answers to those questions (and others) that can push you along the road to greater self-awareness and give you a real chance to change. Asking powerful questions helps you to begin to change those false beliefs.

You may discover that "alcohol makes me more fun" actually means "alcohol makes me more reckless". You may find that "alcohol makes me relaxed" means "alcohol makes me lazy and unambitious".

Once you make those discoveries, you can't unlearn them. And that brings us back to how your beliefs can be flawed and produce the wrong actions.

Let's use the example above to illustrate how powerful questions work in practice.

If you're convinced, deep in your subconscious, that alcohol makes you fun and relaxed, you're sure to keep getting drunk again and again. But once you've admitted that it makes you reckless, lazy and unambitious, you're likely to make very different decisions.

That's self-awareness, subconscious rewiring and neuroplasticity all coming together to help you develop new habits.

When was the last time you stood still for ten minutes and started asking yourself searching questions? If you live on a negative auto-pilot, it's unlikely you have ever done more digging than a simple "why did I do that again". Nevertheless, questions are a great way to challenge our beliefs and start to build a deep level of self-awareness.

If you've ever encountered a toddler, you're probably familiar with "the why phase". From when a child can speak to the age of about five, toddlers incessantly ask "why?" in their desire to learn more about the world around them. It drives many parents crazy.

When you're trying to boost your self-awareness, be that toddler. Keep asking yourself questions, and go deeper until you have nowhere else to go.

When you begin to discover the answers to these powerful questions, you must *own* the answers. Taking responsibility for your actions is essential, and not pass the blame onto others. Shifting the blame won't get you to the root of your problems; it merely gives you a distraction.

An example:

"Why did I drink last night when I know I want to stop?"

Because I was angry and needed some stress relief.

"Why did the anger push me to start on the beers?"

Because there were six in the fridge next to me, and my blood was boiling.

"Why did I feel angry before I drank?"

Because my boss told me to step it up at work.

"Why did that make you angry?"

Because HE's an idiot.

Do you see what you did there?

You've shifted away from using "I" to using "HE". You're now projecting your answers (and your reasons) onto somebody else – your boss.

You must keep coming back to the "I" – to you – for this process to be effective.

If you were going through this conversation with a therapist, they'd take you back to the "I" and continue the questions:

"Why does your boss saying that you're underperforming at work make you angry?"

Because I know I haven't been performing at work and didn't like getting called out on it.

"Why haven't you been performing at work?"

Because I kept getting drunk the night before, I can't concentrate, and I need help staying sober.

It can go deeper still:

"Why do you need help staying sober?"

Because I haven't been able to stop on my own since I started drinking at 14.

"Why did you drink regularly at the age of 14?"

Because I wanted to remove the pain of being bullied at school / dealing with my parent's divorce / struggling to keep up in lessons.

There are differing examples there, but the point is that the further you're willing to head into that rabbit hole, the more you will build your self-awareness. You can reach a point where almost everything in your life makes sense. People often call these moments "epiphanies" or "eureka" and "lightbulb" moments.

These moments don't always come in one session of asking why. Sometimes they take months or even years to unravel, but the important part is that you start. If you feel uncomfortable with what you bring up, seek a qualified therapist to help you through it.

Self-awareness has many layers. The deeper you go, the better your chance of rectifying your problems. Inner child work, which we come to shortly, can take you to the deepest level, allowing you to begin a true healing process.

Asking powerful questions can help you stop leaving important decisions to your subconscious while "rewiring" it to make better decisions!

When it comes to drinking alcohol, you certainly want to ensure you're letting your *conscious* mind make the decisions in the early stages of quitting. That way, instead of just going out on impulse, you might actually think through the pros, the cons, and the likely hungover aftermath.

Remember - your answers will only be as good as your questions. Open-ended questions will reveal much more than closed questions.

For example, on the subject of giving up alcohol, here are two questions you could ask yourself:

A. What am I resisting?
B. Is alcohol negatively impacting me?

Question A forces you to go much deeper into your answers. It's an *open* question. The second question is a close-ended question and invites a shallow "yes" or "no" answer.

Open-ended questions require much more thought. As such, you have to do more soul-searching and really analyse your answers. The deeper you go, the more eureka moments you unearth, the more dots you connect, and the more false beliefs you can leave behind.

Asking open questions is one of the first things professional therapists and coaches are trained to do. Moreover, it's a skill you can develop and use on yourself.

The more self-awareness you have, the more conscious control you can develop. So be that toddler, and keep asking yourself, "why?".

Listening

Do you think you're a good listener?

Many people aren't. Many people are far more focused on thinking what they're going to say next than what a person is actually saying to them.

Over 2,000 years ago, Stoic philosopher Epictetus said, "we have two ears and one mouth, so we can listen twice as much as we speak".[19]

It's a solid piece of advice – especially if you want to boost your self-awareness.

Active listening is something of an art form, and it takes practice. It means actually letting somebody's words soak in while your brain processes them. It means becoming more comfortable with awkward pauses rather than being in a desperate hurry to respond.

Just like reading books, you're sure to pick up valuable insights if you make an effort to hear what other people have to say. You will benefit from their wisdom and experiences and probably feel inspired to ask follow-up questions. That's the art of active listening.

Active listening comes into its own if you attend any form of group therapy, including anonymous group meetings. It's about listening to the similarities in those meetings and not focusing on the differences. Being able to resonate with the stories you hear can be compelling in showing you that you can stop drinking and stay sober.

Focusing on differences in group settings acts as a distraction for your ego to think – "I'm not like them; I don't have to listen to them". The ego is counter-productive for active listening because that person could say a wealth of helpful information, but your ego convinces you that you are not like them, and your focus shifts away. We will learn how to tame the ego later in the book.

Try to be honest about whether you are a good and active listener. American psychiatrist M. Scott Peck said, "you cannot truly listen to anyone and do anything else at the same time".[20] So if you often find your mind wandering mid-conversation, try to work on that. There are rich rewards for doing so.

Pushing Out of Your Comfort Zone (and Taking Healthy Risks)

A surefire way to learn more about yourself (and to become more self-aware) is to put yourself into new environments, do new things and meet new people.

Doing these things forces you out of the comfort of routine, which is especially valuable if your "normal" way is unhealthy or holding you back.

You can summarise this strategy in one sentence: "get comfortable with feeling uncomfortable!"

Sobriety is all about exploring new things, new environments and new people.

There's no need to feel intimidated by this. *Everyone* has to do *everything* they do a first time – and it often leaves them feeling accomplished and fired up for the next time or the next thing.

Sobriety frees up time, money and energy to do all the things you've wondered about doing or "not got around to". And every time you do one of those things, you have an opportunity to pause and reflect on the new experience. How did it feel? How did you behave in that new situation? Is it something you'd like to do again?

What do the answers to those questions give you? More self-awareness!

So go to the group therapy session, book the wing walking experience, start the evening class, and pick back up hobbies that used to inspire you as a child. Sobriety gives you all of those options, and everything you experience feeds into that positive feedback loop:

Build your self-awareness > take positive action > enhance your intuition around what truly makes you happy. Rinse and repeat for best results.

Therapy and Inner Child Work

If you're ready to build a deep self-awareness (and I highly recommend it), it's well worth considering working with a professional therapist.

This is especially relevant if you seem stuck in the same headspace or pattern of behaviour. If that's the case, it could be a good time to call in the experts.

If you've reached a stage where you're *considering* working with a therapist, that's a good thing. It illustrates that you're already self-aware enough to recognise that you're "stuck". Some people struggle to arrive at that point and fiercely resist opening up to somebody.
As a result, they *stay* stuck. So if you're ready to admit that you need some help, you're already winning.

Don't let your flawed beliefs about getting help hold you back. Growing up, my flawed belief was this: asking for help was a weakness. How wrong I was! Finally admitting I needed help and starting therapy was the strongest action I have ever taken.

It's natural to become deeply embedded in our lives and daily pressures. In addition, many of our beliefs – including the unhelpful ones - are deep-rooted.

Therapists complete years of training specifically to assist people in building self-awareness and moving forward from their problems.

They're also skilled listeners. You'll frequently find that they can relay what you're thinking back to you – articulating it better than you could yourself!

A great therapist will ask you questions that nobody else would. Their job is to help you understand why you do what you do, not *tell* you what to do. It's far more powerful to come to your own conclusions at the end of each session rather than waiting for the therapist to tell you what those conclusions are.

A therapist can also help with the inner child work we mentioned earlier. It's essential to ignore the whole "tell me about your father" stereotype. Many schools of therapy, such as Cognitive Behavioural Therapy and Adlerian psychology, don't work like that. However, your early experiences often have a significant bearing on why you do what you do and feel the way you feel. A good therapist will guide you through that.

People often say they had a "good upbringing" but can't remember much of their childhoods. So what was traumatic for them then might not appear that way now.

There's no overstating the power of realisations about your past. For example, you may discover that you were the victim of behaviour you'd dismissed as "acceptable" when it really wasn't. You may uncover a specific turning point that knocked your confidence and self-esteem. You may even remember the trauma you'd "locked in a box" because it was too painful to process at the time.

Deep wounds need deep cleaning. Otherwise, infection creeps in, and the pain comes back with a vengeance. It's the same with addiction. As we said right at the start, you know *what* you do, but the key to making lasting changes is working out *why* you do it.

Regular drinking is often about burying uncomfortable feelings, but they *always* resurface if you don't deal with the cause.

"Just by holding this child gently, we are soothing our difficult emotions, and we can begin to feel at ease. When we embrace our strong emotions with mindfulness and concentration, we'll be able to see the roots of these mental formations. We'll know where our suffering has come from. When we see the roots of things, our suffering will lessen." *Thich Nhat Hanh.*[21]

If you want to give therapy a try, and I strongly recommend it, here are a few tips for finding the right therapist for you:

- Interview two or three before making your choice. Sometimes the chemistry just isn't right. You're likely to have a strong instinct around whether somebody is a "good fit".
- Try to choose a therapist with a few years of professional experience as a minimum. Personal experience can be equally important, but a great therapist will not disclose everything about their past because it can impact how you interact with one another.
- Pick somebody you trust. Without trust, we don't fully open up. If we don't fully open up, we won't delve deep enough for effective healing.
- Ensure they are appropriately qualified. Qualifying as an accredited therapist takes years, including many hours of supervised

sessions. The more experience, the better, but likely the price as well.

Having a therapist can be one of the biggest things you do in your life – it's self-care at its finest. So put those false beliefs aside and give it a go.

"Self-Therapy" With the Power of Journaling

Journaling isn't quite the same as working through your problems with the help of a trained therapist. However, it's a hugely powerful tool and one that many therapists will recommend alongside their sessions.

You can start doing it right away. All you need is a notepad and a pen, but there are plenty of journals you can buy for affordable prices.

A helpful way to work is to record a few daily reflections - both morning and night. This will allow you to build a visual pattern of how your mood changes each day.

With that information, you will be able to analyse what went on for you between those two periods and how it affected your emotions. (Remember – it's your emotions that drive your actions).

Over time, this will build your emotional intelligence, something we will cover more in a later chapter.

Taking the time to write down what's in your mind is therapeutic in itself. The words that end up in your journal hold the key to all kinds of deep insights. These can help to build your self-awareness. You can ask yourself what you could have done better and be honest about the things you didn't like about yourself during the day. On the flip side, you can reflect on what worked and what gave you joy.

There are plenty of sobriety journals out there. Give a few highly rated ones a try, and remember, consistency is key for best results. Journalling can be a great tool in helping you change your inner narrative from negative to positive. Repetition through gratitude, day and night reflections and positive affirmations (more on that later) will help you change how you speak to yourself. When you start talking to yourself positively, this reflects on your actions and how you see the world.

Never underestimate how powerful a consistent journalling practice can be for quitting alcohol, staying sober and maintaining a positive mindset.

Meditation and Mindfulness

Meditation and mindfulness are fabulous tools for unlocking your self-awareness. A recent study estimated that around 275 million people across the world practice meditation.[22] Can that many people be wrong?!

Although meditation and mindfulness are often mentioned in the same breath and are closely related, learning the difference between the two can be key to choosing practices that will most benefit you. One useful way to understand the difference is that "mindfulness is a quality (while) meditation is a practice".[23] That said, people often practise meditation *in order to work on* their mindfulness.

An excellent first aim is to build up to establishing a regular practice that works for you and allows you to meditate deeply. In this meditative state, you can start to observe situations in your life, process them, release your physical and mental tension, and let them go.

This contrasts with how you may suffer from recurring, circular thoughts in your daily life. For regular drinkers, these are often thoughts like "how did I act at my work drinks last night?" and "how am I going to make it up to my family for being hungover on Christmas day?"

Breathwork is another powerful tool, so there's little wonder it plays a crucial role in practices like yoga and meditation. Breathwork improves vagal tone, improves our emotional control, reduces anxiety and stress, and lowers chronic inflammation in the body.[24]

Meditation creates the time and space for you to have a clearer perspective on things. In turn, you can gradually become more *mindful* in day-to-day life, dealing with future situations with more judgement and clarity. It can also teach you quick exercises you can practise throughout the day when you encounter stress, challenges and difficult decisions.

If you want to try a meditation aimed at developing self-awareness, Sober On A Drunk Planet has produced a special meditation just for you. You can access the video and sound recording using the link in the "Free Gift" section at the back of the book. So give it a go – it might just be the tool that helps you stay sober.

Exercise and Nutrition

Self-awareness isn't just a mental thing – it's a physical thing too.

The food we eat and the exercise we do (or don't) significantly impact our mood and state of mind. Later in the book, we will look at the gut-brain axis and how it substantially affects your alcohol-free journey.

However, you don't need science to know that certain things are true. You only need to ask yourself how you'd feel if you shut yourself in a room for a week - with no exercise - eating nothing but greasy takeaways.

Nutrition and movement matter.

Exercise is a transformative tool and one that can be actively used to regulate emotions. In fact, a study showed that "individuals who use exercise to enhance mood report higher scores of emotional intelligence".[25]

People often drink alcohol and take drugs in an attempt to regulate their emotions. The fact you're reading this suggests that you've reached the point where you realise it doesn't work. But eating right and exercising right *does* work.

You've no doubt often regretted agreeing to go out "on a school night" or opening the second bottle of wine. But, have you honestly ever regretted going to the gym, pushing yourself in that spin class, or shaking off a bad day at work with a run?

What does all this have to do with self-awareness?

The more you learn about exercise and nutrition, and the more you act on what you learn, the more you will come to *intuitively* understand what your mind and your body need. That *is* self-awareness.

Over time, you come to understand – on a deep level – how much the mind and the body are interconnected. This can become subconscious, replacing your much less healthy coping strategies. Maybe soon, you'll feel that you "need" to lift weights rather than "needing" a drink!

When you start understanding your mental health is directly linked to your physical health, you have the power to change your mood at any given point. Movement is medicine and feeds an entirely different feedback loop to self-medicating with alcohol (which never ends well).

***

Without working on self-awareness in your sobriety, you're not doing the work that's required to move beyond why you were drinking in the first place. Unfortunately, this is why many people become "stuck" or manage a period of not drinking before reverting back to their old ways (or worse).

With self-awareness as a priority, you give yourself the ability to take positive action on what you learn, allowing you to stop drinking *and* stay sober.

Before you head to the next chapter, I'd like to suggest a quick exercise based on the powerful questions I mentioned earlier.

Ask yourself this simple question:

"Why am I here?"

Travel as far down the rabbit hole as possible, remembering to channel your inner four-year-old. Keep following each answer with another "why?"

question, remembering to ensure that each answer starts with "I……."

Remember though; knowledge is only *potential* power. In the next chapter, we harness that power by learning how to take positive action.

Chapter 2

Dreams Without Goals Are Just Dreams: Goals, Positive Action And Intuition

What are your goals in life? Do they go beyond merely surviving until the next day, the next weekend, the next payday, or the next week off work?

Regular drinkers often find themselves without any true goals. Life becomes all about getting through:

- Getting through the hungover day(s) at work.
- Getting through the "boring part" of the social event before it's time to head to the bar.

- Getting through to the end of the month on what remains of the overdraft limit.
- Getting through until the next holiday – due to living a life you only want to escape from.

It makes for a rather grim existence, regardless of your personal circumstances, your financial status, or the state of your career. Nobody truly aspires to just survive.

As we established earlier, the problem is that drinking fuels that negative feedback loop of drunk > hungover > demotivated > low on energy > drunk again > repeat.

It's no wonder that it stops us from working towards any concrete goals, and it's possible to stay stuck in the same cycle for years. I did.

Then, there is a sudden realisation that life is flashing before your eyes with no notable achievements. Being known as "a legend", "a heavyweight", or "the last one standing" doesn't count. Being able to drink more than your mates doesn't come with a medal or a certificate of achievement!

If you need inspiration to push you towards setting some meaningful goals, consider this quote from Stoic philosopher (and Roman Emperor) Marcus Aurelius:

"Think of yourself as dead. You have lived your life. Now take what's left and live it properly."[26]

Why Set Sober Goals?

The above quote certainly falls into the tough love category, but there's no denying its wisdom. Setting goals helps you to establish new behaviours, guide your focus, and sustain momentum in your life. That's the complete opposite of what alcohol has done for you, landing you with the same predictable behaviours, zero focus outside of getting drunk, and no forward motion in life.

Goals can be small and trivial or vast and profound. Goals can be for the short, medium or long term. It's achieving the small goals that edge you towards achieving the huge ones. Almost always, it's nailing the short-term goals that set you up for achieving the long-term ones.

For example, the short-term goal of "stopping drinking" could be the key first step towards the larger goal of "achieving inner peace".

The "just for today" mindset that's widely promoted in anonymous groups is a powerful tool to help you achieve your goals. Many AA members carry a keyring or coin saying "just for today" to remind them of this. It's all about using energy to focus on the present day, not spending time and energy fixating on the past or future.

Achieving things feels good and sets off a healthy feedback loop. Have you ever decided to wipe a surface in the kitchen and ended up giving the whole room a spring clean or cleared out a drawer and then felt motivated to do all the others too?

Setting manageable goals is as key to giving up drinking as it is to achieving anything else in life. You start with just one clean, sparkling surface and end up with an immaculate home. Start small, and use that motivation and sense of achievement to keep driving you further.

We'll move on to how to set and work towards goals in a moment. But first, it's important to remember that you can (and should) reward yourself for achieving big and small goals. Just don't make an alcoholic drink the reward!

When you're training a puppy, you give them a treat when they exhibit the positive behaviours you're looking for, such as going to the toilet outside rather than all over your home! After a while, they begin to remember and exhibit those positive behaviours naturally. They link the behaviour to the reward.

I'm not trying to say that human behaviour isn't much more complicated and nuanced than puppy behaviour! However, it IS much the same. The thing is, consuming alcohol makes it *way* more complicated than it needs to be.

Think about how the basics of this reward mechanism get twisted when we drink habitually. We reward "happy" with a drink. We reward "sad" with a drink. We reward "depressed" with a drink. We reward "angry" with a drink. We reward "stressed" with a drink.

I could go on.

It's like rewarding the puppy for *every* possible behaviour – with an unhealthy treat - and then wondering why they're causing chaos on a daily basis. (I've been there, I own a puppy!)

The reward-alcohol mechanism will have been used for so long it will be on auto-pilot. Becoming *self-aware* of that link and taking *positive action* to reward yourself with something other than alcohol is how you start to change your neuroplasticity and build new healthier reward habits.

Later in the book, we talk about emotional intelligence. "Rewarding" every feeling with booze is a reliable way to *destroy* your emotional intelligence. It's rewarding yourself for suppressing feelings and failing to learn to deal with them in a healthy way.

And you'll likely suffer far more from the consequences of that than a puppy will!

A SMART Way To Stop Drinking

You may have already heard of the SMART framework for setting goals. It's often used in workplaces, but can also be used to help you to set goals around anything and everything.

The goal of this book is for you to stop drinking alcohol and stay sober. Broken down, this means repeatedly achieving the short-term goal of staying sober each day. (If you're physically addicted to alcohol and suffer withdrawals, it may first involve tapering your alcohol consumption down to zero. Please speak to a medical professional about the best way to detox for your circumstances if you need to taper down.)

SMART stands for:

- **S**PECIFIC
- **M**EASURABLE
- **A**CHIEVABLE
- **R**EALISTIC
- **T**IME-BOUND

Let's apply this to the goal of stopping drinking alcohol.

SPECIFIC:

Stop drinking alcohol for 24 hours.

Being *specific* is crucial in helping us visualise our goals. It's particularly valuable when you quit drinking. Consider this: "stop drinking" doesn't carry the same visual weight in our thoughts as "stop drinking alcohol for the next 24 hours".

The clearer our goals, the easier they are to achieve. In this specific example, the fact that repetition builds habits *and* that we learn from the cycle of achievement and reward both serve to help the short-term goal evolve towards the long-term goal.

MEASURABLE:

If you can't measure it, you can't improve it. That applies to sobriety and personal development.

It's easy to measure whether or not you drink alcohol. However, there are various things you can do to keep yourself accountable. For example, you could join a sobriety group – online or offline. You could download a sobriety app and track sober days, or hire a therapist or coach and be held accountable by them.

You can even venture into social media and start an anonymous sober page to connect with others on a similar journey and to hold yourself accountable. Search for @sober /@recovery /@alcohol-free accounts to follow and be inspired by (or not!). Just be careful not to get sucked into the 'likes' and 'loves' that feed the ego (more on that later).

Seeing the sober day's build-up is rewarding in itself, and celebrating each sober milestone helps to fuel motivation towards the next one.

ACHIEVABLE:

Giving up drinking IS achievable.

MANY people quit drinking each year. Among them are plenty who have lost more than you, drank more than you, had more fights, more arguments and more hangovers.

That's not to belittle the situation you find yourself in – but there's no debating that quitting drinking IS achievable, regardless of where you find yourself today.

REALISTIC:

Is the goal of giving up drinking and staying sober realistic? Yes!

You picked up this book with the intention of making a positive change in your life.

You're no longer in the "should" phase. You're here and you're ready.

The goal IS realistic.

TIME-BOUND:

As we mentioned above, we can keep the timescale nice and simple: 24 hours at a time.

While it would be great to make the initial goal "stay sober for 365 days", it's much easier for our minds to deal with 24 hours of being focussed on not drinking. Again, we want to practice being fully present. Keeping it "to the 'day" helps us achieve that.

A journey of 1000 miles begins with a single step. The same applies to sobriety.

Every sober journey begins with a single day off the booze.

Sober Goals vs Drinking Goals

Earlier in this chapter, I said that many drinkers don't have any concrete goals.

That wasn't strictly true for me.

I had the goal of going to Ibiza every year – to escape from the fact that I really didn't like my job!

Within that broader goal, I had sub-goals too – the ones that society expects for a single male in his twenties:

- Getting a tanned, ripped body (failed every time – alcohol got in the way).
- Shagging lots of people (failed every time – brewer's droop got in the way!)
- Doing as many drugs as possible (achieved that one).
- Coming back feeling like sh*t (this wasn't ever an actual goal, but I smashed it out of the park every time).

I still have holiday goals in sobriety. My main goal is not to drink alcohol and come back re-charged and rejuvenated, ready to take on my *next* set of goals. Those always include being sober, work goals, relationship goals, and any other goals that make me want to get out of bed in the morning.

I wasted a lot of holidays (and a vast amount of money) returning from my downtime feeling worse than I did before I left.

The goals I have now give me *purpose* – something I never found at the bottom of a bottle or in an empty cocaine wrap. Getting sober and having goals has allowed me to find purpose not just at the weekends but Monday to Friday as well.

You don't have to live for the weekend; you can live for a Monday morning as much as you do for a Friday evening!

Millions of Yogis around the world do something very similar to setting goals. They lay out their intentions at the start of a yoga practice. It's a tool that helps them to build awareness of the task at hand, hold them accountable and give them purpose. Remember – you'll never meet a miserable Yogi.

How Do You Achieve Goals? Positive Action

Positive actions are actions that move you towards your goals.

Here's an example of positive action and a negative alternative:

- Say "no" to drinking tonight, and you'll wake up fresh tomorrow morning, ready to visit your family.
- Say "yes" to "just one drink" tonight, and that one drink will likely lead to six. You'll wake up feeling like death tomorrow morning, cancel the family catch-up, and feel guilty about it for the rest of the week.

Unfortunately, there's no magical "secret sauce" that will suddenly cause you to make the right decisions. Motivation *is created by* taking action –

and imperfect action is better than perfect inaction.

As a personal trainer might tell you, "The hardest lift of all is lifting your butt off the couch!". The same applies to giving up alcohol – you must do the work. Nobody's coming to save you.

Cognitive dissonance comes into play again here. Lots of people want to exercise and *know* all the powerful benefits. But they fail to exercise and then feel guilty about it. Likewise, with drinking, people *know* they'll feel better if they abstain. They often have years of evidence to prove that there's zero chance of it ever being "just one or two". But they do it anyway and then deal with days of feeling sh*t, laced with guilt and regret.

The way to overcome that cognitive dissonance is not rocket science. You need to take the correct positive action: to actually *go* to the gym or say "no" to the night out. Doing so will fire up new neural pathways, which will help move you away from your old drinking behaviours and towards new healthier ones.

One thing then leads to another, and it all gets easier – rapidly. It's all about consistency. The first time you wake up fresh, enjoy the day and get a bunch of stuff done, you begin to build that new, healthy feedback loop. It will feel good. You will *want* to do it again.

I'm not pretending that it's a walk in the park. Over time, your brain becomes wired for avoidance. It tricks and manipulates you into doing the *easier* things, which are usually the things you've got into the habit of doing. They're certainly not the things that are outside your comfort zone.

However, remember the "just for today" mantra. That's all you need to get started – the commitment to take the correct positive action that first time.

Getting it wrong is perfectly OK. We all make mistakes, even when our intentions are positive.

But we have an important choice: We can either learn from the mistakes or ignore them (and set ourselves up to make them again and again). You're reading this book, so it's likely you've already had enough of choosing the second option.

I'd encourage you to write a list of positive actions you can take to move you towards your goal of giving up drinking (or another goal in sobriety if you have already quit drinking).

These can include:

- Avoiding the pub on the way home by taking a different route back from work.
- Removing yourself from your friends' group chats, telling them that you're taking a break from going out for your well-being. (This also helps you to avoid getting any abuse for not going out!)
- Avoiding doing the things you always do when drinking. For example, if you sit at home and drink, *avoid* sitting at home. Go for a walk. Read a book in a different room.

Go to the cinema, go bowling, or do anything where alcohol isn't the central focus.

- Telling family that you can't make an event because you are taking time out for your own well-being. (You may find it harder to put boundaries in place with family than with friends - but you need to do both if you want to be successful with sobriety).

When you write down the actions you need to take, you'll often find that the ones that seem hardest are the ones that will move you the quickest towards your goal. So if you can summon the motivation to tackle those first, it's likely to pay off.

Top Tip: You know your goal – stay sober for 24 hours. Whenever you are faced with something that can potentially challenge that, such as being asked out for drinks with friends – ask yourself this:

Will my actions move me towards or away from my goal?

This question will allow you the space and time to think about it – more than you would have done when it was an auto-pilot.

How Action Breeds Intuition

The "end game" of building your self-awareness and taking positive action is to train your intuition. This means getting to a stage where your subconscious makes the *right* decisions. It means having the *right* thoughts and feelings and those feeding into the *right* actions.

It's the exact opposite of what happens when you drink regularly. Instead, you make *bad* decisions subconsciously and remain in the negative feedback loop.

The more you work on your self-awareness, the more you'll be able to take positive action and feel the benefits. Drunk decisions lead to terrible outcomes – drink driving arrests, relationship breakdowns, and declined debit card transactions towards the end of the month.

Intuitive sober decisions lead to positive and exciting outcomes – new job opportunities, healthy new friendships, and the joy of sober creativity.

When your mind, body and soul are in alignment, you begin to consistently make the right decisions. In addition, you hone your intuition and your "gut feeling". (We'll talk more about the gut-brain axis in a later chapter.)

Mistakes happen and are part of the learning process. As you build your intuition, you'll quickly begin to identify any bad decisions you make along the way. When that happens, all you need to do is remember your GOAL. Then, work out what *positive* action to take to move you closer to it.

Let's recap.

There are three steps to follow to reach the goal of living a happy and fulfilled sober life:

Building self-awareness comes first, and you've already started on that. It's self-awareness that's brought you to the point of realising that alcohol no longer serves you.

There's lots of work to do on self-awareness. It's an ongoing process, but the previous chapter showed you how many tools you have at your disposal. The more you understand *why* you drink, the easier it becomes to consistently take the next step, which is:

Taking positive action. This involves not drinking alcohol each day. When you hit each 24-hour goal, you start again the next day and channel your energy and focus again on staying sober. And through the process of taking action, you become more self-aware as you develop along the journey.

Developing intuition happens as your subconscious evolves away from seeing "having a drink" as the solution to everything. Instead, you will build an intuition that runs on a new healthy auto-pilot that makes better decisions with better outcomes.

For example, when you start to build a more evolved level of understanding between your mind, body and soul, you might use exercise and healthy food to deal with a stressful week at work rather than compound the stress with a hangover and greasy food. These are two very different actions with two very different outcomes.

Compounded over time, the results are a world apart. I know, as I have experienced both the positive and the negative feedback loops.

Setting manageable goals (using the SMART framework above) is vital when attempting to stay sober. Dreams of being sober are meaningless without a goal to help you work towards those dreams.

Having that central goal of quitting drinking and staying sober means that a relapse, at any point in the process, needn't be a disaster. Even if a relapse occurs, you're still developing intuition as long as you practice self-awareness and take positive actions.

While learning the three steps above is easy, implementing them and getting them to stick takes time, patience and perseverance.

Here's a tip: Each morning, make it your intention to "not drink TODAY". Make this your ONLY goal in early sobriety, and drive all of your energy and focus into it.

By focusing every bit of your attention on that goal at the start of every day, you give it the recognition it deserves. In turn, that will help to drive your actions throughout the day.

I can assure you that – with time – the daily "not drinking" goal will require far less of your energy and power. As your self-awareness and intuition builds, you'll be able to work on all the other things on your list of goals.

Next, we look at emotional intelligence and how working on yours can turbocharge your self-awareness, the actions you take and the intuition you develop.

Chapter 3:

The Sober Child: Emotional Intelligence And How To Apply It

Emotional intelligence is the ability to recognise, interpret and regulate emotions.

It's important to note that this doesn't just mean *your* emotions. True emotional intelligence is also about empathy and how well you understand the emotions of those around you.

A high level of emotional intelligence is a desirable trait - in personal relationships and (increasingly) in the workplace. There are many online tests that will "score" you on emotional intelligence, often resulting in an Emotional Quotient (EQ) score – the empathy equivalent of an IQ for intelligence.

Why Emotional Intelligence Is Key To Your Sobriety

Emotional intelligence feeds directly into our self-awareness and – in turn – our actions and intuition. Our emotions drive our actions, so the more we can *recognise*, *interpret* and *regulate* our emotions, the more chance we have of taking the *right* actions. And, as we've established, that's a crucial key to stopping drinking and staying sober.

An excellent way to understand emotional intelligence is to first think of a young child. It's clear that they operate with a rather limited range of basic emotions while they begin to make sense of the world around them. This process involves feeling emotions which are alien to them to start with. With time, they learn, don't learn, or learn incorrectly how to *recognise, interpret* and *regulate* their emotions.

I have yet to see a grown adult crying uncontrollably and throwing a tantrum in a supermarket. That's proof that, at a basic level, we have all emotionally matured to some extent!

There's a range of scientific theories around how many "basic emotions" there are.[27] For example, American phycologist Paul Eckman names six: sadness, happiness, fear, anger, surprise and disgust. The Neuroscience and Psychology Institute at the University of Glasgow trims this list down to just four, grouping fear with surprise and anger with disgust.

Thinking back to the child, before too long, a parent can begin to recognise Eckman's basic emotions in their offspring. They will learn to distinguish anger from fear and happiness from surprise. They may see how disgust manifests itself when they first feed the child broccoli or cauliflower!

As we grow up, we begin to understand that there are many other nuanced and complex emotions that go beyond the basic six. "Happiness" could mean experiencing pride, awe, bliss, satisfaction, or many other things. "Anger" could be a manifestation of frustration, envy, powerlessness, discomfort or anxiety.

Just because we come to understand that there are dozens of different emotions, that doesn't necessarily mean we develop the emotional intelligence to recognise them – in ourselves or in others. And if we can't recognise them in ourselves, we can't regulate them.

This takes us to the heart of why honing your emotional intelligence is a powerful tool for boosting self-awareness and achieving your goals. If you understand the emotions driving your actions, you're more likely to stick with the positive feedback loops instead of reverting to the negative ones.

First, however, we must deal with a problem:

Alcohol is *terrible* for emotional awareness. It's terrible because so many people are conditioned to "treat" almost every emotion with alcohol.

If you're "angry" and accustomed to having a drink to "calm down", you're probably not even coming close to working out if "angry" actually means feeling frustration, envy, powerlessness, discomfort, anxiety or one of many other complex emotions.

Alcohol is a numbing agent that prevents us from truly recognising our emotions and taking a healthy course of action to deal with them. An emotion comes along, and rather than sitting with it and dealing with it, we bury it with alcohol. And it's not just alcohol – people often do the same with drugs, food, sex, gambling and other things.

Have you ever needlessly eaten another snack to try and remove that feeling of boredom or ordered more online shopping you didn't need? They are prime examples of numbing the emotion of boredom without alcohol. It's worth noting that cross-addictions can be common when you give up alcohol, swapping it for another addiction like shopping, sex, drugs, relationships, food, gambling, etc.

When you stop drinking, become self-aware of your habits and think to yourself, am I in the same cycle of substance > regret > repeat that happened with alcohol? This will help you understand any potential cross-addictions (food was a big one for me personally).

This practice of burying every undesirable emotion is summed up in Anonymous groups when they say someone is "irritable, restless and discontent". The only way past this is to learn how to recognise our emotions and develop healthy ways to deal with them.

Quitting alcohol is just the start; all those emotions must be unravelled and worked through in sobriety to prevent relapses from occurring.

If you're getting a sense that you wouldn't score very highly on an EQ test, don't blame yourself for it. The breadth of your emotional vocabulary may well have been defined in your early years.

Earlier, we discussed how plenty of people would readily say they had a "good upbringing" and perhaps dismiss the possibility that they experienced any trauma in childhood.

But what if crying was met with, “toughen up”, “that’s enough”, or “what do you have to be sad about?” What about the children who grew up around parents who themselves had never really evolved beyond six simple emotions?

Not every child develops the ability to label complex emotions. This is a phenomenon known as alexithymia. In reality, emotionally immature parents will raise emotionally immature children, and a lack of emotional intelligence can be traced back through generations.

I lacked emotional intelligence for 17 years – throughout my entire drinking career. Alcohol made me emotionally immature. It never gave me a chance to work on my EQ score.

The good news is that we have the power to develop more emotional intelligence at any age. It’s essential that we do. If we can’t identify our true emotions and regulate them, we’re far more likely to hit the big red “f**k it” button whenever we encounter an emotion we're not equipped to deal with.

So how do we get past that point?

There's a reason this chapter is called "The Sober Child."

When people stop drinking – sometimes for the first time in decades – they are left to deal with all of the emotions they used to bury with alcohol. In some cases, if they lack emotional intelligence, they struggle to even put a name to those emotions – other than the basic selection described above.

For example, they may feel "angry". However, they don't know they're actually feeling jealous, powerless, inadequate or embarrassed.

It's entirely possible that you have *never* truly experienced emotions in adult life because you have always used alcohol to forget and "de-stress". Constantly numbing yourself, weekend after weekend, produces a zombie - not a human being ready to take on the world and make their mark.

Emotions all feel very new in early sobriety - and can also feel overwhelmingly scary. It's a true "child state". As such, the risk of relapse is high. So the path of least resistance is to go back to the one thing that makes the emotions go away – alcohol.

This is why it is crucial to work on your emotions and learn to untangle them without using alcohol. If you don't do this, they will resurface in the future – possibly with horrific results.

Emotional intelligence matters because it allows us to navigate life with less stress, less emotional reactivity, and fewer unintended consequences. It's key to replacing negative feedback loops with positive ones.

The "irritable" emotion is one you're sure to encounter on your journey to a life without alcohol. It's a complex emotion that's often discussed in sobriety circles.

It frequently arises when a regular weekend binge drinker encounters the first "big night out" that they need to say "no" to. Then, a powerful feeling of "FOMO" (Fear of Missing Out) descends.

With that feeling comes irritability, known to some as "the wine witch" or "the alcohol devil". Others call it "addiction".

If you've not sat through that feeling before, it will prove incredibly uncomfortable. You'll feel bored, angry - like it's all deeply unfair. You'll convince yourself there's *nothing* else that you could be doing while your friends are out. (This – of course – is a false belief. There are thousands of other things you could choose to do).

Your brain will then start playing tricks on you, wanting you to pick up that first drink. It will say things like "one will be alright".

There's a really easy way to make the uncomfortable feeling pass.

Give in.
Go out.

Press the big red "f**k it" button.

The trouble is, there's only one outcome from that. You're straight back into the negative feedback loop. Drunk > hungover > full of regret > miserable for the next week.

If you want something different, you HAVE to DO something different. And that will bring up emotions you don't like – at first. (The good news is that it will likely *never* feel as hard as it does the first time.)

Avoiding hitting that "f*ck it" button is what you need to work through. It WILL feel uncomfortable. You have to get used to the feeling of being uncomfortable because that's how we stay sober and grow in all areas of life.

When you initially went to school, you might have found it scary. But eventually, once you'd been enough times, it was no longer as scary. It soon felt normal.

Sobriety is the same; it feels uncomfortable to begin with until one day, it feels normal.

You have to become self-aware of that feeling of irritability. You need to *recognise* it and learn what *positive actions* you can take to *regulate* the emotion that sets it off instead of pressing that big red button.

The scenario described above is one I encountered over and over again. It led me to relapse – over and over again.

I really struggled with what I labelled as "boredom". But boredom isn't an emotion. The *feeling* of irritability leads to boredom (which is a belief that there is "nothing to do"). That process gives the addicted mind a reason to self-sabotage, and the next thing you know, you're out getting drunk.

What's different for me now?

Over time, I've learned to *recognise* that something doesn't feel right. I then *interpret* that as the feeling of irritability. I then *regulate* that emotion with positive actions.

The more you do this, and the more you come to understand your emotions, the more your emotional intelligence improves.

Using the above example, which we'll call "Friday night FOMO", there are various ways you can regulate the irritable emotion with positive action.

Personally, I might go to the movies or book an 8 pm exercise class. I might even go to the pub for a few hours – but with a solid exit plan and a clear resolve to only drink alcohol-free drinks. I can react *positively* to the emotion of irritability without drinking or drugging, and still get an early night and wake up fresh on Saturday morning.

Exercise is a powerful tool for changing how you feel. (I may have mentioned that a few times already!) Movement is medicine because it can completely snap you out of a negative emotion and gift you a positive one in its place.

Alcohol, on the other hand, can take a positive emotion (a good week at work) and turn it into a negative one. It can guarantee you a stressful weekend because of the depression caused by enduring a crippling hangover and achieving nothing.

Physical activity has the power to improve how we regulate emotions. It decreases cortisol[28] (the stress hormone), which interferes with our ability to think straight. It also releases feel-good chemicals (endorphins and dopamine), leaving our brains in a better state to regulate our emotions.

The ability to "turn that frown upside down" comes almost instantly with exercise.

Building your emotional intelligence seems really straightforward when it's written down. However, when you've spent years using alcohol as a numbing agent, it can *take* years to untangle that and feel aligned again.

How To Recognise, Interpret And Regulate Your Emotions

Here's *how* to improve your emotional intelligence and better *recognise*, *interpret* and *regulate* your emotions.

Stage 1: Recognising Emotions

First, you must work on how to recognise emotions – something that's much more difficult than many people realise. After all, if you can't tell which emotion you're feeling, how will you ever learn to interpret it, let alone regulate it?

Emotions can manifest themselves in all kinds of ways – both mental and physical. For example, anger can feel like your blood is boiling and can emerge in seconds. It can range from mild anger to violent rage. Being fearful could make you feel sick to the stomach, and feeling happy could leave you with a smile.

The Emotions Wheel below shows a range of basic emotions, with more complex emotions in the outer rings. It will help you to *recognise* emotions so you can move onto the stage of *interpreting* them.

To see the full-size Emotions Wheel please visit: www.soberonadrunkplanet.com/emotionswheel

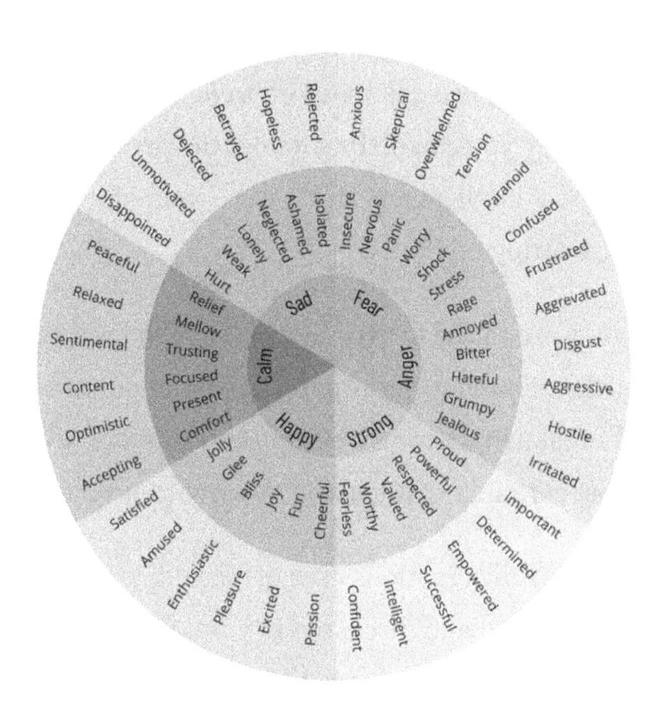

As mentioned above, if your emotional intelligence is lacking at this stage, you may well find that you only readily recognise the basic emotions in the middle. The emotion wheel is a powerful tool to

help you move beyond that. For example, you feel "fear", but are you, in fact, overwhelmed, anxious, or insecure?

Stage 2: Interpreting Emotions

Once you've *recognised* the emotion you're experiencing; you can move on to *interpreting* it. How easily you can do that comes down to emotional intelligence, and – yes – your childhood has a bearing on that.

If you were raised by parents with a high level of emotional intelligence – parents who understood and regulated their own emotions – this skill will almost certainly have passed down to you.

But if the only emotions ever displayed, acknowledged and discussed in your childhood home were the basic ones, it's no surprise that you will struggle to readily interpret emotions in your adult life. Similarly, if showing emotion was actively avoided – something that's very common – you will find this process more difficult.

To *interpret* what an emotion actually means for you, you will need to step back from being reactive. Instead, you will need to create space to feel that emotion and think before taking some appropriate action to deal with it. Then, using the tools mentioned in the self-awareness chapter, you can create that space to interpret them. The alternative is an ill-judged and inappropriate action (which could well be deciding to drink).

Delving into the more complex emotions can really help. Learning that you're actually frustrated, envious or bitter gives you far more to work with than just thinking you're angry.

You won't get it right every time. Sometimes you may interpret an emotion incorrectly and take the wrong action as a result. For example, feeling nervous may indicate you care deeply about something, but it's possible to mistake that for feeling anxious and fearful.

Getting it wrong, learning from your mistakes and moving on is all part of the process. Often there are many layers to our emotions, and getting to the root of them takes time. Therapy and inner child work can help enormously.

Stage 3: Regulating Emotions

The third stage is key to improving your emotional intelligence (and, in turn, your EQ score).

Emotional regulation has two unhealthy extremes. You may well be able to recognise one of them in yourself. You'll *certainly* be able to recognise them in plenty of people you know!

At one end of the scale, you have overreactive people. These people react to things almost instantly – often with anger and aggression. There's no time between them feeling an emotion and reacting to it – often in an unhealthy or irrational way.

At the other end of the scale are those who shut down emotionally. Ironically, they are sometimes people who CAN recognise and interpret emotions – but they are not skilled at regulating them.

Shutting down emotionally may – to some – seem more desirable than flying off the handle. Some people (and even some cultures) encourage it, but it's unhealthy and a form of self-sabotage.

For example, imagine a friend keeps borrowing money from you and failing to pay it back. At the over-reactive end of the scale, you could break their door down and lose the plot. Probably not the best thing to do.

Shutting down emotionally could mean saying nothing. As a result, you'd replay the problem in your head, not resolve the situation, and use vital day-to-day energy that could be spent on more productive things. You'd also inadvertently send a message to that friend that they could continue to treat you unacceptably.

By emotionally shutting down, you continue to live with the emotion *and* all the negative consequences of not dealing with it. That's exhausting.

Thankfully, there's a healthy mid-point on the emotional regulation scale: creating the space to feel and think before acting in an *appropriate* way. This could mean calmly but firmly stating your position – and then, once again, evaluating what to do once you hear your friend's response.

Here's a personal example of how emotional intelligence works in practice, encompassing all three steps: *recognising*, *interpreting* and *regulating* emotions.

I used to drink (a lot) on Thursday evenings after work. I now know that it was largely brought on by the fact I was really unhappy in my job.

Unfortunately, the drinking (and the resulting hangovers) masked the emotion of unhappiness. It took me years to *recognise* it. Only after a year of sobriety was I able to identify how unhappy and unfulfilled my job was making me feel.

I went through a process to *interpret* why I was unhappy. I was sober. I had a job that paid well. I had a great relationship with my family again. An outsider looking in would have assumed I was thriving.

Despite this, the overriding emotion that I felt - every single working day – was unhappiness. I finally accepted that despite the money and the security the job gave me, it still made me miserable.

Getting sober allowed me to be more in tune with my emotions. I realised that I was in the driving seat of my life rather than the passenger seat. (Interpreting emotions was very new but also extremely empowering).

After *recognising* that I was unhappy in my job and *interpreting* the fact that it was because the actual work I did wasn't in tune with my new, sober self, I was ready to move to the final stage: *regulating* that emotion of unhappiness.

Shockingly, it took me 12 YEARS in total to get to that point! Alcohol had been numbing my emotions all that time!

I was finally able to take the right, positive action by looking for work that aligned with who I was and where I wanted to go.

It all seems so simple now. But millions of people spend years, if not a lifetime, stuck in an unhappy cycle due to the inability to *recognise, interpret* and *regulate* their emotions.

Emotional intelligence is hugely influential. You can apply it to any feeling you encounter as you go through your life. The more you do so, the more you build your intuition and begin consistently making the right decisions – for yourself and your future.

In terms of staying sober, understanding your emotions helps you not to react to them by drinking. Instead, you regulate them and respond with safe alternatives that will help you to avoid drinking altogether.

We come on to understanding cravings and triggers in the next chapter. Again, emotional intelligence is a key to understanding what can emotionally trigger us to relapse.

Don't be surprised if you find it difficult to *recognise, interpret* and *regulate* emotions. Unfortunately, the inability to do it is incredibly common in people who've become used to using alcohol as a coping mechanism.

If this resonates, a therapist could be of great help to you. They will guide you through understanding your emotions and reacting to them in healthier and more positive ways.

If you feel stuck and struggle to get past emotions such as anger and sadness without turning to alcohol, it could be the perfect time to get help from a professional.

A therapist's job is to act as a mirror, ask those powerful questions, and help you reach the deep levels of self-awareness that may elude you on your own.

Whether you work with a therapist or commit to boosting your emotional intelligence solo, you will notice the change in yourself over time. You will start to pick out your emotions, see how your behaviour evolves, and how it feeds into your intuitive actions.

And that's when you will start to consistently choose the positive feedback loops rather than the negative feedback loops.

Resentments And The Art Of Letting Go

"Resentment is like drinking poison and waiting for the other person to die". Malachy McCourt.[29]

It's worth singling out resentment because it plays a vital role within the twelve-step program. It's impossible to ignore how powerful the twelve-step program has turned bitter, twisted alcoholics into forgiving, loving, caring, sober role models.

You don't have to like AA to appreciate that it does work and has worked for a long time. Overcoming resentments is at the heart of its success.

Resentments do two things:

1. They stop you from being fully present, as you are always thinking about the past situations that caused the resentment (for example, not getting that promotion at work).
2. They take up a lot of energy. You're constantly thinking about the resentment, and you wind yourself up, which also causes physical stress.

Learning to overcome resentment allows you to be fully present in your day-to-day activities. It also means that you don't use vital energy in situations you have no control over.

Letting go of resentment is an art form. It takes time, but you quickly learn that holding grudges doesn't move you forward in life. Instead, holding grudges keeps you in a negative past you cannot control.

I had hated everyone by the time I stopped drinking. I hated the fact they were all ahead in life. I deleted social media because I hated seeing people happy. Everything was a reminder of how sh*t I thought I was.

I resented everyone and everything because I was so deeply miserable about my own life. Alcohol and other drugs felt like the only temporary solution to that feeling, even though I was quickly heading for rehab.

That particular feedback loop is incredibly toxic - and becomes a self-fulling prophecy. I *thought* I was worthless, so I *became* worthless. It was all driven by resentment, which drove me to drink. The cycle was extremely difficult to break until I got sober and started to work on my resentments (this is step four in the twelve-step program).

Resentment is a strong emotion and one that leads to relapse due to the incredibly short-lived relief that alcohol provides us from feeling "mistreated". I lived in that cycle for a long time. As such, understanding resentment was a massive part of my recovery.

When you start writing down, on paper, who and what you resent, you quickly spot a pattern: Alcohol turns you against the world! What a tragic place to live when you hate everyone and everything. (I am sure you will see this in other people who complain and moan about everything!)

Below is a table you can use to copy and write down your resentments. Write down who you resent, why you resent them, the emotions it brings up, and what you think letting go will achieve.

Take your time – people in AA can take years to finish this step before moving on to the next because they have built up many people and places they have resented over the years. This is an incredibly therapeutic exercise – especially if you have been carrying a lot of unnecessary baggage.

Who or what do you resent?	**What was the cause of the resentment?**	**What emotion does this make you feel? (Use the wheel.)**	**What do you achieve by letting go of the resentment?**
Wendy	She got promoted over me at work.	Mistreated and sad.	I can move forward, ask for feedback as to why I didn't get the job, and look to improve for the next opportunity that arises.
Tommy	He is doing really well for himself – nice car, nice house, gorgeous girlfriend.	Fear that I am not good enough.	I can move forward and concentrate on my own life – worrying about where others are in life won't help me move forward in mine.

It's worth noting that you can always produce a new list – even in sobriety. Since I stopped drinking, I have been resentful of people still. It comes and goes, but the difference is I can recognise it, interpret what it means for me, and then let it go. It is often a reflection of how *I* feel (frightened, angry, sad etc.) rather than anything they have actually done.

Usually, the person you resent will have no idea how much time and energy you waste on resenting them! They will likely never even know that there was a problem in the first place!

Moving past resentments is a massive step towards freeing yourself from things you have no control over (such as other people, places or things). It will also give you power over one of the most powerful emotions that cause relapse and the ability to manage it without hitting the bottle.

Once you have become self-aware of resentment, you can take positive action to stop it from impacting your sobriety. Over time, you will build intuition that makes this exercise second nature.

Signs You Are Emotionally Maturing

It's all well and good doing these exercises, but as we mentioned under the 'Measurable' for SMART goals – if you can't measure it, you can't improve it.

You could take an emotional intelligence test online and compare your results over time. Or you could take time to reflect, using the points below, to see whether you are emotionally maturing (or not):

- You understand that some people only engage in negative behaviours and realise that you don't need to join them on that self-destructive path. This could mean saying "no" to the Friday night session.
- You are responsible for how you respond to people around you and practice regulating your emotions. For example, when your mates try to get you out for "just one drink", you opt to stay in instead of pressing the big red button.
- You understand that people make their own minds up about the life they lead. You get that it's not your place to change or control people or to force your beliefs onto others.

When you get sober and enjoy its many gifts, you want to tell the world how amazing it is, but you quickly understand you can't make people change – they must want to change for themselves. This book provides guidance to help you change; it's entirely up to you whether you use it or not.

- You can tolerate differences of opinion. (This also helps to weaken other people's egos - more on that later). It's healthy to disagree – you don't have to be a sheep, and you certainly don't have to let disagreements ruin the rest of your day/week/month/year.
- You create the space and time to respond, thinking things through before making informed decisions rather than being reactive.
- You practice healthy emotional boundaries and can say "no" without feeling guilty or frightened of what others might think. You stop being a people pleaser and start to put your sobriety above everyone else.

- You can let sh*t go that would have made you turn to alcohol. That's real maturity.

If you start seeing some of these in your day-to-day sobriety, you are well on your way to improving your emotional intelligence score!

***

What emotion are *you* feeling when you decide to hit that big red "f**k it" button and reach for a drink?

You can use the emotion wheel above to help work that out. Then, once you've identified how you feel, spend some time working out *why* that emotion comes up for you.

Processing your emotions is not an exact science. Circumstances will rarely be the same every time. But the idea is to get you thinking consciously about your emotions and what might trigger you to drink. And that brings us nicely onto the next chapter.

Chapter 4:

People, Places And Things: Understanding Cravings And Triggers – And How To Deal With Them

Sometimes it's relatively easy not to drink. Sometimes it's much harder.

If you've been drinking for any length of time and find yourself craving alcohol, that's completely natural. The science of how alcohol works on the brain explains why.

Alcohol floods the brain's reward circuits with dopamine[30], often referred to as the "feel good" neurotransmitter. (It's worth noting that many other things cause your dopamine levels to increase exercise, sex, food, achieving goals, going shopping, or doing anything else you enjoy. Most of these are much better for you than alcohol!)

The problem is that, over time, alcohol depletes your natural dopamine levels. As a result, the brain adapts to the unnatural dopamine flood and produces less of it.

With less dopamine around whenever you're not drinking, you're left craving more alcohol - because you think it will make you feel better.

Triggers are different to cravings, but they're closely linked. In fact, triggers are the things that *lead to* cravings.

Triggers come in all shapes and sizes: being around certain people, being in certain environments, and being subjected to day-to-day stresses and strains. Even a particular smell (including those not related to alcohol) can act as a trigger.

Here's a typical example: 4 pm on a Friday may be a triggering time to think about alcohol. Perhaps everybody's beginning to talk about which bar to head to after work. That trigger then leads to a craving. The "Friday feeling" that many people refer to is nothing other than a craving for alcohol - being set off by the simple fact that it's Friday!

It can push you along a path of physical irritability *and* mental frustration: You *want* a drink, but you also want to stay sober.

This is the time to think back to what you learned in earlier chapters: You must become **self-aware** of the triggers and cravings so that you're in a position to take **positive action** to avoid a relapse. The more you do this successfully, the more you build intuition and start trusting your subconscious to make those decisions for you.

Once again, it's a positive feedback loop vs negative feedback loop. The alternative is drink > regret > repeat.

There's another thing that's valuable to understand about cravings, triggers, dopamine and addiction. A scientific study on the mechanisms of relapse acknowledges that "the reinitiation of drug seeking after abstinence occurs before exposure to the drug itself, and is instigated by environmental cues, thoughts or stressors."[31]

Drug addicts often say that the chase of scoring drugs and the ritual of preparing them produces as much of a high as taking the drugs themselves. A parallel for drinkers is planning the night out, deciding where to go, and getting ready.

Science supports this. A study shows that the release of dopamine can be brought on by nothing more than the *expectation* of consuming a substance.[32] While that may seem unnecessary, it's really useful to know when it comes to identifying your triggers.

Over time, your brain will have established strong neural pathways associated with drinking (and possibly taking other drugs). It's essential to work on removing those strong links between drinking alcohol and various people, places, and things.

The dopamine that keeps you craving is released before you even take the first gulp. So with that in mind, the objective is to avoid those people, places, and things heavily associated with boozing.

Just like training a puppy, you need to positively reinforce *new* behaviours – and it's especially important in the early days.

Let's look at some common triggers to become self-aware of.

People (Friends, Family And Colleagues)

Nobody is suggesting that getting sober means you need to avoid everybody you've ever had a drink with. But your drinking (or drugging) buddies will inevitably be high-risk triggers for you. Often, groups of drinkers and/or drug takers share a collective lack of self-awareness and emotional maturity.

There's no getting away from it: You're more likely to relapse if you spend a lot of time around people you've always got drunk with.

If you're serious about quitting drinking, a good mantra to keep in mind is that "the friends that mind don't matter and the friends that matter don't mind."

You will know - better than anybody - which people in your life will be the most troublesome triggers when you're trying not to drink alcohol. My drinking and drug buddies were a big problem for me, but it could be certain work colleagues, family members, your football crew, or the mum's group at school.

Boundaries are crucial and as relevant to family members as to friends and colleagues. So even though you might find it harder to say no to family members, your sobriety has to be above everyone else – including your family.

You'll probably need to take more extreme action in the early days to avoid triggers than you will after some solid sober time. It will take time for new habits to form and new neural pathways to be created, so patience and perseverance are key. This could mean saying no to social events in the short term. (This will quickly help you to work out which friends mind and which friends matter!)

You will also find it surprisingly easy to find new "sober buddies" via social networking sites and in-person groups. The fact that getting sober is an increasingly popular trend means that there are plenty of kindred spirits around.

When you decide to venture back into scenes where drinking is prevalent, plans and strategies are essential. You could be held accountable by a sober buddy or a best friend (although the latter may prove a challenge if your crowd loves to drink).

Visualising and planning ahead will help ease any alcohol-free anxiety you might have around attending a boozy event. Seeing what non-alcoholic drinks are available beforehand will stop you from feeling pressured when you are at the bar and already anxious. "Failing to plan is planning to fail" is a great saying to remember when planning sober nights out in places where you know booze will be flowing.

Plan an exit strategy, think about what alcohol-free drinks you will enjoy, and be ready to set boundaries. Say "no" and refuse to stand for any abuse.

People who say things like "oh, go on" and "why are you being boring?" are not the kind of people you want to be around when you're making a positive life change. Remember that you're doing this for your own well-being.

Sobriety is your only goal - so don't give other people the power to derail it.

Places (Pubs, Clubs, Holidays, Sports Venues, Funerals, Weddings, And More!)

As explained above, your brain makes strong neural reward links related to your habits over time. So, for example, visit any place you strongly associate with drinking, and your brain will likely start to release dopamine and make you crave hard.

If you want something different, you have to do things differently. You need to break the habit of being yourself to start a new alcohol-free life.

For example, I used to drink in a pub where I worked and lived. I also bought drugs from people in that pub, and almost all my journeys involved going past it.

For six months, I stopped driving past – even if every journey took extra time. I had to break that connection and help re-wire my brain to live a new, sober life.

I still drive past that pub occasionally, and my instant thoughts are still around alcohol and drugs. The difference is that I don't *act* on those thoughts anymore. The reward link is no longer there.

How do you deal with triggers linked to places?

Take different routes, and avoid the local pubs you used to drink in (at least in the early days). Be self-aware of the fact that you're making a conscious effort to rewire your brain. This will help to weaken the strong associations you've built up around alcohol. And they could be powerful indeed – built up over years or even decades.

Find some new places to spend some time. Suggest that friends meet you in a coffee shop, not a pub. If they say "no", it may be time to get some new friends!

The key is finding new places not associated with your old patterns of behaviour. The good news is that there are plenty of them. Once you're free from having to only choose places that serve alcohol, you quickly realise how many other alternatives exist.

Things (Literally ANYTHING)

Dealing with triggers around people and places is challenging enough. Unfortunately, there are many other things that could get those pesky neurons firing, such as smells, times, tastes, and activities.

For some ex-drinkers, the smell and taste of alcohol-free beer are too much of a trigger (although it's worth mentioning that, for many, the availability of a wide range of alcohol-free drinks makes things easier. Only you will know where you stand on that).

Paraphernalia can be triggering: cigarettes, pint glasses, wine glasses, beer mats – even bank notes for cocaine users!

Going on holiday is often a big trigger. Even *booking* a holiday can be a trigger. The association of relaxation and enjoying yourself could be enough to get the dopamine flowing, triggering you to crack open a bottle of wine to celebrate.

Many sober people particularly struggle with attending their first wedding. The association between weddings and drinking to excess is an incredibly strong one!

I've spoken to ex-drinkers triggered by barbecues, sunshine, and certain songs. You may not be able to list all your triggers right now, but you can be *sure* that you'll find them out over time!

This rewiring process takes time. Sometimes it will feel easy, rewarding and exhilarating. Many people experience the "sober honeymoon" or "pink cloud" in the early days of quitting.

But don't be fooled. Subconscious conditioning can run deep; even after years, you can find that something trivial triggers a craving.

How To Cope With Triggers

In the early days, the simplest way to cope with triggers is to say "no" to the things you know will present challenges.

Once you've built up some sober time and worked on your self-awareness, you'll ease yourself back into social events and other things you did when you were drinking. You may find that you come to enjoy them even more, especially sports and hobbies.

Another essential thing to consider is that stress is often the biggest trigger.

Obviously, you don't have full control over the stressful situations you encounter. But you can avoid life-changing events that are certain to increase your stress levels. For example, when you're in the process of quitting drinking, it's probably not the best time to move house, get a puppy (trust me on this one) or change jobs.

However, stress in small quantities is healthy. Only when we go through stressful situations can we learn about ourselves and become more resilient to those situations in the future. So, in your early days, it's about taking baby steps with stress and not going all in on everything. I have attended many AA meetings and group therapy sessions to understand that stress is one of the biggest causes of relapse, whether you are 15 days or 4,526 days sober.

Never get complacent.

I almost learned the hard way after being sober for a number of years and deciding to publish my first book, move house and get a new puppy all at the same time! I might have given in if I hadn't published a book about giving up alcohol and used the tools mentioned in this book.

Clearly, you can't avoid every trigger unless you hide in a cave. Even if you did, your mind would probably find some triggers of its own! With that in mind, here are some strategies for coping with the triggers you *can't* avoid:

- **Seek the support of others.** Partners, friends, sober buddies, and members of online communities can all help you to work through situations where you're resisting temptation. A surprising number of newly sober people find themselves on their smartphones at weddings, getting support from others online while they're struggling not to give in.
- **Sit with the feeling.** Sometimes it's just a case of "riding it out". For example, you

may be used to seeing off social anxiety by sinking a couple of drinks at the start of a work event. What you'll find is that that feeling passes *anyway*. And it gets easier every single time.

- **Remember your reasons.** Get into the habit of reminding yourself of your reasons for giving up alcohol. Perhaps keep a note on your phone, or in your bag, with a list of the reasons why you wish to stay sober. You could even get a tattoo!
- **Find distractions.** Cravings pass. Think of a series of activities you can turn to when you're struggling. Don't underestimate the power of a ten-minute walk around the block or a quick wander around a bookshop or record shop to treat yourself with the money you would have spent on booze.
- **Play it forward.** This is particularly useful if you have those (very common) "it'll be OK if I just have one or two" feelings. Think about what's happened on all the other times you planned to just have "one

or two". Then, think about how you'll feel tomorrow morning if you break your streak of sober days.

- **Just go!** If a situation is becoming too much for you, just leave. It may help (and reduce your stress levels) if you lay the groundwork in advance and tell people you need to leave early. But in reality, it doesn't matter at all. The people who stayed out drinking likely won't remember – and even if they do, they'll be too hungover to care!

An exercise to end this chapter: Get a notepad and keep it by your bed. You can list out across three columns: People, Places, Things.

Start writing a list of those instances you can remember that act as triggers, and build the list over time. You are building **self-awareness** of your triggers so you can take **positive action** to stay sober and develop your **intuition** for future events.

These are just examples (there might be an element of truth in them) to help you:

People	Places	Things
Tommy – drinking buddy	The Tavern (Local pub)	Smells that remind me of holidays (certain cleaning products, weirdly!)
Wendy – drinking buddy at work	My Nonnas house (Being Italian, wine was always on offer and on show)	Little button bags you get with a new shirt/trousers remind me of a drugs bag
Uncle Stan at Family gatherings (Yes, family can be triggering!)	Going on holiday (literally anywhere!)	Alcohol-free drinks (they remind me of alcohol versions – everyone is different though)

In the next chapter, it's all about the big "I am."

It's time to talk about the ego.

Chapter 5:

The Sober Ego

– Understanding And Taming The Ego

The ego is the self-interested "I" that develops from childhood. Our experiences of the world feed into our thoughts. In turn, these thoughts begin to construct beliefs, which determine how we interact with the world.

The trouble is that the ego can get *way* ahead of itself. It can quickly become overinflated, distorting our reality and making us behave as who we *think* we are and not as who we *actually* are.

But let me reassure you: As you will see in a moment, it's not necessarily your fault if your ego makes you behave like you're the centre of the universe. You're not necessarily to blame if almost every sentence you utter starts with "I..."

Society conspires to make people that way.

That said, basing reality on a false sense of self is dangerous if left unchecked. It's not good to be blind to your ego and any false beliefs you may hold about your own worth to the world.

Let's examine why the problem arises and what to do about it.

Modern capitalism may as well have been custom designed to make egos run wild. Everyone wants more. Everyone wants *better*. It's actively encouraged and inescapable. Advertising and social media have a lot to answer for.

The rat-race lifestyle has been a thing for decades. It's on steroids these days.

You're certain to encounter plenty of egos in pubs, bars and clubs. Many of them attract (fairly or unfairly) people known for their particularly outsized egos: the bankers, the estate agents, and the social media “influencers”. They all meet up in bars and clubs. Egos follow other egos, all determined to “out ego” each other!

Alcohol and drugs are kryptonite for the ego. It’s a bad enough beast *without* the addition of substances. When we drink, we can also develop “alter egos”. Some people completely change character when they’ve had a few. This is known as the “Jekyll and Hyde” effect – where the person's sober character is entirely different from the ‘monster’ they become when they get drunk. You might even resonate with it!

There’s “Wendy the Wino”, known for an ability to drink her body weight in wine. Believing herself to be the “life and soul”, she’s loud, brash, and a constant pain.

And propping up the bar over there is “Tommy Tequila”. He’ll snort a line of salt before smashing a tequila shot into his eye. He thinks he’s a legend, but he’s actually an arrogant, self-righteous idiot.

While he's having fun, he's ruining the evenings of plenty of people in the vicinity.

There are certain behaviours that point to an over-inflated ego. Bitching and moaning about other people is a big one, and you hear a *lot* of that in the pub. Others include arrogance, redirecting blame, holding grudges and resentments, never being wrong, interrupting people, and taking credit for other people's successes.

The ego can distort our own level of importance. This leads to us putting ourselves above other people and becoming unteachable.

It's a recipe for disaster.

You're reading this book because you want help. That's a good thing because you've put your ego aside in order to learn. But it's still there waiting to catch you out.

The ego likes to be comfortable. Anything that makes it *un*comfortable is seen as a threat. (That's perhaps why "Tommy Tequila" is inclined to say, "what you looking at?" to anybody glancing disapprovingly at his drunken antics!)

The key to succeeding in life and pushing through challenges is always to accept that you're the student and never to assume you're the master. There are infinite things to learn about life on earth, but the ego likes to think it has nothing left to work on.

Next time you receive feedback that you don't like, ask yourself a simple question: Do you *really* have nothing to learn from that feedback, or is it your ego, desperate to defend itself?

Thinking back to my own drinking days, I'm now self-aware enough to know that my unhealthy sense of self (my ego) put up a LOT of barriers. It prevented me from empathising with others, learning about the world, and recognising opportunities. I made far too many decisions based on an illusion of who I *thought* I was, not who I *truly* was (or, deep down, wanted to be).

The ego plays a huge part in why people relapse. Finally, they reach the point where they think they're "OK". But it's the ego talking.

Have you ever tried a diet, lost weight, and immediately returned to your old ways? This is the ego getting ahead of itself (as it tends to do). It thinks the goal was obtained when you actually had much further to go.

So your ego reverts to what was easiest. Eat what you want, when you want and don't worry about going to the gym. This false sense of self has inflated again, and it thinks it knows better. So you end up back to that point where your trousers are too tight, you wonder how you put it all back on again, and you call your personal trainer for help - AGAIN!

You see the same process happen with people who give up drinking. They get compliments, they fit into the new trousers, they look younger, and they have more money, but for those who don't manage their egos from overinflating and creating this false sense of self – they start to believe they are alright, they can drink. It won't be as bad as before.

A few weeks later, they cave in. The cycle repeats of hangover > regret > repeat until they stop themselves again (this could even be you!).

Stopping drinking without doing the hard yards on self-awareness and intuition can leave you in a "dry drunk" state (a term often discussed in Anonymous groups).

Imagine "Tommy Tequila" once again. He could stop consuming alcohol but still remain arrogant and self-absorbed, with no desire to please anybody but himself.

It's perfectly possible to be sober and still be a dickhead.

Once again, this is modern society at work. It's natural for the ego to try to take control again. We live in a competitive, "look at me" world. To some extent, we *need* our egos if we want to get ahead in life and be seen and heard.

Your ego will *always* be a part of you. What matters is how you manage it, tame it, and use it to your advantage so you can stop drinking and stay sober.

How To Manage Your Ego And Use It To Your Advantage

So how DO you manage your ego? Here are some effective ways:

Watch and Listen To Yourself

Work on becoming hyper-aware of the things you say that focus around "I", "me", "my", "mine", and "myself". What are you truly saying?

If you catch yourself bitching about somebody, ask yourself what's really going on for you to cause you to belittle them. Are you perhaps fearful that they may be doing better than you?

The ego *hates* fear, insecurity and jealousy. The ego doesn't like to feel uncomfortable. But it's often enough to merely observe, watch and catch when the ego is coming into play. This subdues and tames it.

Once more, self-awareness is key. Without self-awareness, you're allowing your ego to take complete control. Do you find people who are clearly "all about me" endearing? It's highly unlikely, but if you're ruled by your ego, you will be one of those people.

Remain Humble

There are many ways to be humble. They include helping others without expecting a reward, practising gratitude, daily journaling, and listening more than talking.

Receiving and processing (rather than arguing with) feedback from others is also hugely influential in keeping yourself grounded.

Recognise your flaws and admit when you have made a mistake.

Be Teachable

Remember – you're the student, not the master.

Everybody you pass in the street knows a bunch of things you don't and is better at certain things than you.

One particularly nasty thing that the ego does is work to prevent you from getting the help you need. It can actively stop you from living a life to be proud of.

Do you need to go to therapy? Do you need to go to rehab? Do you need to admit to a family member that you could do with some help? Your ego could hold you back from doing all of those things, and may well have already done so.

Before getting sober, I was terrible at accepting feedback when I worked in the corporate world. Instead, I would bitch, moan and find excuses.

Then it came to bonus day, and I never had a bonus that matched my ego's expectation. So my default ego response was to look for other jobs. Surely someone else would pay me what I thought I was worth?!

Only now do I know that much of that feedback was fair and correct. If I'd actually listened and taken advice, I would have become a better person much sooner.

There's nobody you can't learn something from.

Avoid Ego Battles

One-upmanship and "keeping up with the Joneses" is a disease of modern capitalism.

There's little duller than competitive conversations about house values, salaries and new car purchases, but it's all part of our "bigger and better" culture. Unfortunately, even if you don't initiate these conversations, the ego will usually get dragged into them.

The best way to diffuse these situations is to be as non-reactive as possible when they do come up. *Never* look to initiate them yourself. If a conversation fails to fuel the other person's ego, it will soon fizzle out.

Don't Talk About It – Do It!

The way to impress people isn't to talk about your achievements; it's to achieve them.

Even better is to achieve the things that matter to you and not *care* whether or not anybody is going to be impressed. A choice you always have is "to be or to do". The right choice will give you focus and keep you grounded.

Don't Chase "Likes"

Social media platforms are designed to be addictive and make you feel loved. They're *intended* to provoke emotional reactions, and the "likes" and "loves" keep people coming back.

Sober communities, in particular, can be incredibly supportive. But don't get carried away with chasing likes, loves and cuddles. It can become addictive and over-inflate your sense of self.

The ego really gets off of social media. So be careful how much of it you allow.

Present the Facts

Egos don't like to back down from being "right" – even when they're clearly wrong. It's bonkers.

Don't get dragged into pointless disputes – with your own ego or with those of others. We all have Google in our pockets – we can use it, find the correct answers, and move on.

Make POSITIVE use of an Alter Ego

Not all alter egos are as tiresome as "Tommy Tequila" and "Wendy the Wino". However, we all need a *little* bit of ego to navigate the world we live in. A healthy alter ego that helps navigate stressful and challenging situations can serve us well – so long as it's carefully managed!

In his book "The Furious Method," Tyson Fury, the world's best heavyweight boxer, discusses how his alter ego - "The Gypsy King" - helped him reach such heights. Every time he put on the gloves, this different person arose. He was confident, fearless and full of bravado - precisely what you need to win at that level of boxing.

But Tyson Fury is a husband and family man – not somebody obsessed with fame and wealth.

As long as you don't *become* your alter ego, it can be used as a powerful tool in work situations, social situations, and other times when you need to "come out of yourself" a little more. Just remember to check in on your ego to ensure you're not falling back into old ways.

Don't be a Tommy Tequila or Wendy the wino.

Understanding how your ego works is central to boosting your **self-awareness,** which keeps you teachable and helps prevent you from putting yourself above others. Choosing **positive actions** to deal with your ego will help keep you grounded and your **intuition** on point.

As you go through life, your ego WILL flare up. It takes work and persistence to deflate it.

Here is a quick exercise to finish this chapter:

Next time you find yourself bitching and moaning about somebody, slow down and really think about how you are speaking about them and the context of the situation.

In that situation, ask yourself, what is it that I am unhappy about in myself?

Because it will always be the true meaning of why you are bitching and moaning about other people.

In the next chapter, we talk tactics. A sober life means dealing with the bad days, the good days, the challenging days, and the easier days. It also means doing it all without an unhealthy “prop” to “help” you through.

It’s time to really focus in on the things that help you *stay* sober.

Chapter 6:

Old Ways Won't Open New Doors. Practices To Help Prevent Relapse And Strengthen Your Sobriety

You can always count on life delivering plenty of ups and downs. As we've said, sobriety is easy some days and much harder on others. That applies as much in established sobriety as in early sobriety.

Not drinking *does* become much more natural over time. You can go weeks or months without even thinking about it. But unexpected stresses and not-yet-dealt-with triggers can appear from anywhere. It could be anything - from a bereavement to that first sober trip to an all-inclusive resort.

Let's look at some ways to really strengthen your sobriety and help prevent a future relapse.

The Attitude Of Gratitude

Gratitude works. I will explain why in a moment.

The capitalist, rat-race lifestyle keeps us wanting more. It's part of our conditioning. We buy a house and immediately notice if the neighbours have extensions, conservatories, garden offices, or newer cars parked outside.

However long we saved for that house, it's suddenly not quite enough.

The ego – unsurprisingly – gets fully on board with this, and the "more more more" cycle continues.

It's no wonder so many people turn to alcohol for its numbing effects. But it creates a toxic mess. You're unhappy that you don't have all the "more" you wish for, *and* you consume a substance that robs you of your potential. You end up being unhappy and starting to resent everyone and everything.

I plunged straight into my own rat-race adventure as soon as I joined the working world. I was constantly blinded by the future and never satisfied with what I had at the time. It didn't even occur to me to thank my parents for everything they'd done to get me to that point.

I had a roof over my head, a secure job and healthy family and friends. Yet, I was never grateful for any of it. Instead, I looked at others and envied what *they* had. I never felt like I had sufficient "shiny things".

Little did I know that gratitude held a simple key to being much happier - and less inclined to drown my sorrows because I didn't have the things I "had" to have.

Gratitude works much better than booze. It's a completely free tool that staves off envy, dissatisfaction, and entitlement. These strong emotions can cause relapse at any stage of sobriety, not just at the beginning.

Research demonstrates that practising gratitude can "support greater health, happiness, and wisdom in ourselves and our communities".[33] For example, a study of a group of people completing a simple daily gratitude exercise showed that they were "significantly happier and less depressed". The effect continued even months after completing the exercise.

Gratitude is a crucial part of twelve-step programs. Those programs have helped turn some of society's worst drunks and addicts into compassionate sober heroes who have completely turned their lives around. That's too powerful to ignore.

I've practised gratitude ever since I got sober. It keeps me grounded, humble and grants me the gift of perspective. I can't pretend that material things haven't crept back into my life. But it's gratitude that helps stop "drunk dickhead Sean" (and his big ego) from re-emerging.

When you become grateful for the things you *do* have, all of your other "wants" become less important. As a result, they become less able to impact you emotionally. That's a big deal because it means you're *way* less likely to hit the big red "f**k it" button and relapse.

So how do you practise gratitude?

There are two simple steps[34] involved:

1. Taking time to acknowledge the things you are grateful for.
2. Learning that the majority of the things that you are grateful for come not from within yourself but from other people or things – your family, your pets, the world or the universe.

A great way to start is by developing the habit of listing three things you are grateful for every single day. You can do this in any way that works for you. Popular methods include doing it in your head while you brush your teeth in the morning or using a notepad (or gratitude diary) last thing each night.

Here are the kind of things you might put on a daily list:

- I'm grateful that I woke up sober.
- I'm grateful for waking up without a hangover / a headache / an urgent need to run to the bathroom(!)
- I'm grateful that the sun is shining.
- I'm grateful for the love and support of my family.
- I'm grateful that my children are happy and healthy.
- I'm grateful that I have hobbies to look forward to.

In the above list, note the absence of things like "I'm grateful for my BMW" or "I'm grateful for my big, shiny Rolex." This is because superficial and materialistic gratitude doesn't hold much power at all.

Note that the examples take into account the second step – being grateful for things that come from *outside* yourself.

It's important to practice deep, meaningful gratitude. "I'm grateful for my cat" is a relatively meaningless statement. Think about *why* you're grateful for your cat –the fact he makes you feel comforted and safe – or maybe even the fact you don't need to worry about vermin in your home!

Deep gratitude breeds deep, strong emotions.

However you decide to practice gratitude, consistency is vital. It's another one of those positive feedback loops that rewards repetition. And it works – the science and the experience of millions around the world who practice it demonstrates that.

Embracing "JOMO"

We've all heard of "FOMO" (Fear of Missing Out). JOMO (Joy of Missing Out) is FOMO's enlightened cousin. It's infinitely better.

Fear is a strong emotion and one that can tempt us to join the big night out. But what are you *truly* going to miss out on? Forgetting what you talked about and then *worrying* about what you talked about? The hangover? The overspending? The goals you didn't do any work on because you'd sapped all your motivation?

Compare the "JOMO" alternative: You wake up knowing exactly what you did the night before. You're up early, you're not hungover, and you're ready to get stuff done. You have more money in the bank rather than less. You're motivated to do whatever you truly want to do – whether that's working on a life-changing project or indulging in a hobby.

Both FOMO and JOMO play into feedback loops. I'll leave it to you to work out which is positive and which is negative! Over time, a repeated decision to set boundaries, say "no", and be the driver rather than the passenger can start to drastically change the direction of your life.

This *doesn't* mean you never go out! The difference is that you start to go out when you *want* to rather than when you incorrectly think you *need* to.

To relate this to everything you've learned so far:

- Being **self-aware** means knowing that if you go out without a sober plan, you're likely to repeat the patterns of behaviour that led you to read this book in the first place.
- Taking **positive action** (or inaction, in this case) means saying "no", resisting peer pressure, and doing what's right for YOU.
- Building **intuition** involves learning from the times you make the right choices: "I felt great last weekend; I want to feel great again."

Limiting Beliefs vs Positive Affirmations

We've already talked about the importance of asking yourself powerful questions.

Here's one for you:

Unless you heavily depend on alcohol and need a medically supervised detox – **what is your excuse for not getting sober before?**

Most regular drinkers will have a quick answer: "I've been going through a divorce." "Things have been tough at work." "My relative has been unwell." "I've been really stressed!"

All of those are limiting beliefs and – frankly – they're nonsense. Alcohol has never made a divorce more straightforward. Alcohol has never made it easier to thrive at work. Alcohol doesn't make it easier to care for sick relatives. And as is well documented and scientifically proven, alcohol makes people far *more* stressed and depressed.

As long as you are alive, no matter your life situation, you hope to turn it around, whether it's drinking, drugging, bankruptcy, a bad breakup, the death of a family member or any challenge you face.

Be grateful that you still have hope. Because if you are dead, you have no hope.

Even if you are in prison, you have hope. If you are in rehab, you have hope. If you're reading this book after relapsing for years, you have hope.

Hope is the catalyst for making change.

Limiting beliefs stop us from making meaningful changes. They feed our internal monologue – the thoughts that become our beliefs. But thoughts are all they initially are.

You have hope, and you have a choice.

You can tell yourself, "I'm a worthless alcoholic," and you can become one and stay one.

Or you can say to yourself, "I am capable of recovering from alcohol and will live my best life," and do just that.

Stay with me if this seems annoyingly simplistic. Clearly, it's not quite as simple as just thinking differently and changing overnight. But it's not actually much more complicated than that. All you need to understand is that limiting beliefs are a huge factor in remaining in a negative feedback loop around alcohol.

"I'm not good enough. So I'm going to get drunk."

"I can't do this work. So I'm going to get drunk."

"I won't ever live up to my brother or sister. So I'm going to get drunk."

All of the above are limiting beliefs. You need to recognise them, be self-aware around them – and change them. A great way to do that is to replace them with positive affirmations.

The first thing I was taught in rehab was to stand in front of a mirror, look myself in the eye, and repeat a series of positive affirmations.

If the thought of that makes you cringe, be reassured that I cringed too. Standing in front of a mirror saying things like "I am confident and able" seems particularly ridiculous when you don't believe a word of what you're saying.

But the thing is, people almost always arrive in rehab at their lowest point. My inner monologue was dangerously negative by then. I was constantly telling myself I wasn't good enough – and that kept me in a negative feedback loop. If you tell yourself you're unworthy, unlovable and incapable, it *will* become a self-fulfilling prophecy.

Here are some examples of limiting beliefs and the positive affirmations you can use to counter them.

Limiting Belief	**Positive Affirmation**
I'm a negative person.	I'm a positive person.
I'm not loved.	I'm capable of being loved.
I'm boring without alcohol.	I'm more than enough when sober.

I'm not confident.	I'm confident and able.
I won't ever be successful.	I'm allowed to achieve anything I work towards.

If you think about it, you'd never talk to a friend or loved one the way you talk to yourself. But unhappy drinkers often stay trapped by limiting beliefs for years. Those beliefs may have been embedded as far back as childhood (and, once again, it's well worth doing the work to get to the bottom of *that* rabbit hole).

So, dare to stand in front of the mirror and kickstart the process of rewiring your brain. The quality of your life depends on the quality of your thoughts, so work hard to kick the negativity into touch. Rinse and repeat daily for maximum results.

I don't deny cringing and objecting when I was first introduced to positive affirmations, but they work. If they didn't, I would still be drinking and telling myself how useless I am.

You will become **self-aware** of your own limiting beliefs – remember, if you find an excuse for not doing something, that is your limiting belief. Ask yourself when confronting your own limiting beliefs – is it true?

When you become aware of those excuses, you can take **positive actions** to help you reach your goal of not drinking and staying sober.

These skills will play out in practice, and you will build on your **intuition** to catch yourself with future excuses and almost start asking yourself subconsciously – is it true? Then, finally, you can move past excuses and get sh*t done automatically.

Look Into The Crystal Ball Of Drinking

Drinking alcohol - Is one of the few things in life (along with paying taxes and death) that we know with a great deal of certainty has VERY repeatable outcomes. You don't need a crystal ball to tell you what will happen but looking into the future is a great tool to help you stop reliving the same nightmare on auto-pilot.

One phrase you see a lot on sobriety forums is "play the tape forward". It links to the skill of visualisation.

Visualisation ties into self-awareness. It's all about learning to consciously think ahead, to help you navigate around triggers and tricky situations.

Working on your visualisation skills can keep you out of a lot of trouble.

For example, say you're on your third week of sobriety, and your friends try to tempt you out for "a couple of drinks".

Play the tape forward.

Has it ever been just a couple? Of course not. You probably have years of solid evidence to support the fact that it's more likely to be an all-nighter.

What happens after that? An argument? A fight? A hangover? Forgetting what you said but knowing it was embarrassing? A drained bank account? A day or two off sick from work? Possibly all the above?

Visualising these likely scenarios will help you to take the right *actions*. That *may* mean saying "no" to the invitation (and indulging in the Joy of Missing Out).

Strategies can include having an "exit plan" to ensure you emerge from the situation sober. For example, give yourself somewhere you need to be after two hours and make it somewhere you must drive to. Or decide in advance to leave as soon as your friends are on their third drink – you'll probably find you want to by then anyway!

It can be helpful to focus on emotions when you "play the tape forward". By visualising the situation in advance and thinking about how you will *feel*, you begin to train your brain *before* you end up in the situation. So, encourage yourself to imagine the embarrassment of being the drunkest person at the wedding or the fear of stumbling shakily into work on Monday morning. It's a powerful thing.

The great thing about visualisation is that it works both ways. So as well as playing the tape forward around the things you don't want to do (and the things you don't want to happen), you can also visualise all the positive outcomes from making better decisions.

Let's use the wedding as an example: You could visualise waking up fresh the morning after, remembering every moment - including all the times people told you how *well* you were looking! You could visualise the person who *was* the drunkest person there and how *they'll be* feeling in the aftermath. And perhaps – just this once – you could indulge your ego and visualise people being impressed by your new-found sobriety.

While visualising, you're making some powerful neural connections. You're helping your brain begin to link pleasure with NOT drinking. You're starting to repair the years of faulty thinking.

And – perhaps most importantly – you're making it way more likely that you'll get through the wedding proudly sober rather than embarrassingly drunk.

In his book "How Champions Think," sports psychologist Dr Bob Rotella talks about a common trait shared by some of the world's most successful sports stars. They often *visualise* winning an event over and over before they actually pick up the silverware. All the nerves have been lived through already, many times in their own head. The actual event becomes a lot easier, and they're able to finally pick up that trophy in reality.

Visualising getting through a boozy event with no hangover can see you picking up *your* "sober trophy" for making it through 24 alcohol-free hours.

So being **self-aware** that you have potential hazards along the way will allow you to visualise and plan ahead.

Knowing potential hazards will allow you to plan around them and take the appropriate **positive actions**, remembering your primary goal – to stay sober.

When you have been to a few events and used the tools, you will start to build a sobering **intuition** from how previous events had gone. You will have a sense of what worked well, what didn't and when it's the right time to leave to protect your sobriety.

Stop Letting People Live "Rent Free In Your Head"

You HAVE to stop worrying about what people think.

It drains your energy and leaves you anxious – two things that can push you back towards the negative feedback loop of drinking.

Nobody really cares whether or not you drink alcohol, yet many people going sober become fixated on how to explain it. The reality is that people often don't notice or ask – and if they *do* ask, they soon *stop* asking.

If it bothers you, you can always prepare an answer for the "why aren't you drinking?" question. "I like the person I am when I'm sober" is usually more than enough to stop people digging.

Worrying about what people think goes way beyond worrying about how they might judge your decision not to drink. Breaking free from what other people think is key to evolving as a person.

It's extremely common for people to place their happiness in the hands of what they *think* other people think about them.

It's a ridiculous concept.

We *vastly* overestimate how much time *anybody* spends thinking about us!

Here are two transformative things to realise:

1. People have their own sh*t to deal with and are fighting their own battles in life. They simply don't have that much time to think about you.
2. Happiness is an inside job. You cannot give other people the power to determine whether you're happy or not.

Learning these things can help you quit drinking. Remembering them in the long term can transform your life.

Progress Not Perfection

Have you failed if you stay sober for 99 days and get drunk on day 100?

It may feel like it, but you absolutely haven't. In fact, you've managed to stay sober for 99% of the time over that period.

The most successful people in the world are the ones who just keep persevering, regardless of what they are faced with. They get back up when they have been knocked down.

You can learn a lot from a relapse. So it's a great time to start asking some powerful questions:

- What's going on for me that I decided to drink?
- What triggered me to open that bottle of wine? (get your notepad out!)
- What caused me to want to drink?

Evaluate, re-apply yourself, and move on. Give yourself some compassion. It's difficult enough becoming sober on a drunk planet when everybody seems obsessed with alcohol. So don't beat yourself up if you fall - get back up and get on with it.

The important thing *not* to do is use your perceived "failure" as an excuse to immediately revert back to your old ways and revel in self-pity.

If you relapse, you have a choice: You can stay in relapse mode and keep hitting the "f*ck it" button, or you can choose to start your sobriety again the next day. You have the power to decide what action you take. One is positive, and the other is negative!

You are **self-aware** that relapse isn't the end of the world. Nothing about sobriety (or life) is perfect. Instead, it's a great learning opportunity and one that we have all suffered (countless times!).

Understanding that its progress, not perfection, will allow you the space to heal from relapses and take **positive actions** to get back on it (in sobriety terms!).

The more you know and do, the more your **intuition** will grow, and every relapse will give you a nugget of information to help you overcome future ones.

Avoiding Procrastination

How many times have you said, "I'll quit after Christmas?" or "I'll go on a health kick after the holiday?"

It doesn't happen, does it?

If you want a better life, why are you putting it off?

There will always be a birthday do, a wedding, a barbecue, friends coming over, or some unexpected event you feel the need to celebrate or commiserate.

Just start— one day at a time.

If you fail, "fail forward". Then, get back up and start again. You're still building your self-awareness and learning how much better it feels to wake up full of energy rather than full of regret.

Do you really want a better life, but "not just yet"? If you're honest with yourself, that doesn't make any sense.

Alcohol-Free Accountability

Accountability is incredibly powerful when giving up alcohol. It's the cornerstone of the sponsorship model used by Alcoholics Anonymous – and it works.

If you were determined to commit to a solid month of exercise and fitness, you could try to do it yourself with willpower alone. Alternatively, you could hire a trainer and sign up (and pay) for a "body transformation package".

With the second option, you're far more likely to go the distance. You've created accountability. You won't want to let the trainer (or other group members) down. You won't want to waste the money you've spent. And you'll have a professional keeping you on track and encouraging you.

It's the same with quitting drinking. It's not impossible to get sober on your own, but the reality is that it's harder.

It's worth trying to find some support and accountability. The harsh truth is that you're unlikely to get it from family, friends, or colleagues – especially if they're the people you'd usually drink with.

Thankfully, you have plenty of options. Join a sober group, exercise group, see a therapist, a coach or a psychologist. Just do something that takes you away from your old habits.

Getting involved in groups can help tremendously with many of the things already discussed in the book, including active listening and understanding the emotions of others. Better still, they allow you to meet like-minded, sober, and authentic new friends.

You can join our very own Sober on a Drunk Planet group by visiting www.soberonadrunkplanet.com/community. We will happily support you along the way. The group is full of people who have already "walked the walk" and have experienced sobriety "on the other side". The group is home to many different people with different experiences - and they'll be able to answer almost every question.

Being **self-aware** that results are better achieved when being held accountable by someone, something or some group – should encourage you to take **positive action** and start being held accountable to more people than just yourself. Plus, it's more fun!

By using therapy, sober apps, and joining sober groups, you will find which ones work and which don't and be more selective to be in groups that give you energy and help you grow. That's developing **intuition**.

***

You're now armed with plenty of strategies to strengthen your sobriety. In the next chapter, we talk about another strategy: getting your mind and body working properly together – which makes *everything* easier.

Chapter 7:

Strong Body = Strong Mind. The Importance Of Movement And Nutrition In Sobriety

Exercise and nutrition are fundamental to the health of the body and mind, but the way these things are presented to us is depressingly one-dimensional.

TV ads and marketing campaigns always seem to focus on losing weight and gaining muscle. They hint at a simple equation: If you exercise and eat well, you'll look good. And if you look good, people will like and admire you.

It's not as simple as that. These campaigns play directly to the ego – and we've talked about how the ego works!

The problem with this simplistic focus on exercise and nutrition is that it skips past the many other life-enhancing benefits. Many of them are crucial to building strong sobriety and avoiding relapse – so that's what we focus on in this chapter.

Alcohol is a poison. It's not remotely nutritious. It actively damages the mouth, the throat, the oesophagus, the stomach, the liver and the bowel. A one-off drinking session is enough to "damage the mucous cells in the stomach, and induce inflammation and lesions". [35]

Grim.

Drinking alcohol is also a reliable way to compromise any exercise regime you attempt to stick to. The hangovers dictate that most runs, workouts and exercise classes become discarded good intentions. And then the negative feedback loop kicks in: lethargy, no motivation, and a cycle of shame that leads straight to the pub.

The Damage Alcohol Does To Your Health

Let's look at some frightening ways alcohol damages the health of "chronic drinkers". Before we start, we'll define that term. "Chronic drinker" may make you think of a homeless alcoholic who starts every day with a can of Special Brew. That's not the case. It refers to anybody who exceeds 14 units of alcohol per week and doesn't have regular alcohol-free days.[36]

A LOT of people are chronic drinkers but don't realise or admit it to themselves.

Here's some of the damage being done:

- Alcohol disturbs the effective processing of a whole host of nutrients. These include vitamins A, B, C, D, E and K, minerals such as magnesium, calcium and zinc, and Omega 3 acids.

  We need sufficient vitamins and minerals to boost our immune system, help cells and organs do their jobs, and support normal growth and development.

So they are essential.

- Alcohol damages the gut, causing conditions such as intestinal permeability (leaky gut), irritable bowel syndrome (IBS) and an overgrowth of bacteria. This can occur with "even moderate drinking". The laundry list of related symptoms includes constipation, diarrhoea, bloating, fatigue, anxiety, pain and low mood.

Is it any wonder drinkers struggle to exercise?

- Alcohol sends your brain chemistry into a tailspin. It messes with – among other things – dopamine (the "feel good" hormone), serotonin (the neurotransmitter that regulates your mood), and GABA (an amino acid that helps control stress and anxiety).

None of that is stuff you really ought to mess with.

- Alcohol disrupts hormones and disturbs immune, nervous, and endocrine systems. This can cause issues with adrenaline levels, mood disorders and problems with sleep.

And we've not even talked about what alcohol can do to the liver yet.

Alcohol-related liver disease includes alcoholic fatty liver disease, alcohol hepatitis and cirrhosis. Unfortunately, none of these are a good thing either!

Nutrition and exercise are two sides of the same coin. It's crucial to get a grip on both. Contrary to popular belief, you can't eat what you want and exercise to compensate. Food choices go far beyond just calories consumed.

Comforting though it may be to buy into that myth, it makes as much sense as believing that you can get as drunk as you like without a hangover, so long as you drink two cups of water before bedtime. It's just not true.

After putting the work into giving up alcohol, it's easy to delude yourself that everything else will take care of itself.

It's not the case – and it's a trap that I fell into.

When I stopped drinking alcohol and doing cocaine, my body craved sugar. Loads and LOADS of sugar. Sugar is addictive and a significant component of most alcoholic drinks I used to consume.

Sugar produces massive dopamine surges, just like alcohol and drugs.[37] It can become a "cross addiction", and that's something to be wary of. I'll come back to sugar shortly.

In sober communities, people often justify overeating as being "not as bad as drinking alcohol". This misses the point. Replacing one addiction with another shouldn't be the aim. Remember what we said earlier in the book about that feeling of being "irritable, restless and discontent?"

The aim is to eradicate that feeling – not just find new ways to try to temporarily bury it.

The Life-Changing Benefits Of Exercise For Sobriety

Donning my personal trainer hat, I'd strongly recommend getting into exercise and fitness. It can be one of the most rewarding activities in sobriety. It can fill your weekends, give you a purposeful reason to wake up in the mornings, and get you used to working towards goals.

Getting fit also delivers a whole host of life-changing benefits that are integral to strong and long-lasting sobriety. Here are some of them:

- Exercise boosts your energy levels by increasing the amount of oxygen you breathe in – which is measured by your VO2 Max.[38] If you inhale more oxygen, you have more energy available to use.

Nobody's ever wished they had *less* energy! VO2 Max is used by athletes to assess their overall fitness level. You don't have to be an athlete to measure it or get started in improving it. Even taking a walk each day will help.

- Regular physical activity improves insulin sensitivity.[39] This helps the body control its sugar levels, which reduces cravings. You will see why this is so important shortly.
- Exercise releases endorphins, which improve mood and reduce stress. (I've *never* known a single client to turn to me after a workout and say they didn't enjoy it!)

  Endorphins are vital to sobriety – positively reinforcing that you don't need alcohol to have moments of pure joy is like seeing your puppy poop outside for the first time (rather than the living room carpet again!). It's a behaviour > reward link you want to keep on repeating, and it keeps fuelling that positive feedback loop.

Plus, the natural highs don't come with the negative feedback loop of hungover > regret > repeat, which keep us feeling miserable.

- Regular exercise can help improve the part of our brain that is linked with regulating our emotions. In turn, this helps prevent relapse, as discussed in the Emotional Regulation chapter.

  Instead of taking anger out on somebody, join a Muay Thai class or do some hot yoga. Afterwards, you *won't* carry the same emotions you did at the start. You will see emotional regulation at work.
- Exercise gets the blood pumping around the body. This improves liver and kidney function[40] and aids the body in removing toxins. Contrary to popular belief, you can't just "sweat them out!"
- Working out (and eating a healthy diet) can help to overcome fatty liver disease.[41]

- Exercising helps you to build natural confidence. While it's true that looking leaner, stronger and younger does play to your ego, there's no denying that it's something everybody wants! If you feel more confident, you feel more at ease in social situations. This means you're far less likely to drink alcohol as a way to ease your discomfort.
- Science proves that exercising improves your cognitive function and problem-solving skills.[42] Living a sober life involves consistently making the right decisions and choosing the best actions. A clear mind helps!
- Exercise makes you physically stronger. People often underestimate the difference it makes to be functionally strong – not having to grunt with effort when picking something up or doing up a shoelace!

When you drink, you can become sedentary, losing muscle mass and bone density. Weight and resistance training can reverse that, making you notice the existence of muscles you didn't know you had!

- Developing skills, pushing through pain thresholds and beating personal bests help build physical and mental resilience. So you go into each session pushing yourself to come out 1% better each time. This is the main principle of getting fitter and stronger – progressive overload. But you can also apply the principle of progressive overload in all parts of life.
- Exercise can help you beat insomnia and improve your quality of sleep.[43] I cannot overstate just how transformational it is to get seven or eight hours of restful sleep regularly.
  Alcohol seriously disrupts sleep anyway. Heavy drinking reduces sleep quality by 39.2%, and can also make sleep apnoea worse.[44]

Getting good sleep fuels a positive feedback loop of its own. When you wake up rested, you're more likely to do *more* exercise and eat more healthily (instead of groggily ordering a takeaway and collapsing on the sofa).

- It's medically proven that exercising regularly reduces your risk of coronary heart disease, stroke, type 2 diabetes, bowel cancer, breast cancer, early death, osteoarthritis, depression and dementia.[45] That's quite the list.
- Exercise (specifically yoga) can help you to overcome and manage your response to past trauma.[46]

The list goes on and could easily be much longer.

Movement truly is medicine and goes far beyond just losing weight and gaining muscle.

Opportunities to exercise are everywhere. There are no excuses! (If you do find yourself coming up with excuses, it's worth re-reading the section on limiting beliefs in the previous chapter!)

So get involved at the gym, go to a class, go for a walk, join a sports team, download an exercise app, or find some yoga videos on YouTube. Do whatever it takes to get your heart rate up and your lungs pumping.

If you want to build some accountability and have the budget, a personal trainer or a strength and conditioning coach can help guide you towards your goals. Group-based training is another option because you will still have that sense of accountability in relation to the other group members.

Remember the importance of positive action. Get your exercise clothes ready, and set an alarm the night before. Be held accountable, and make sure you take the first step.

The saying "the hardest lift is lifting your butt off the couch" is true. Just as nobody regrets getting sober, nobody ever regrets doing exercise (unless they tried to exercise during a hangover!).

Also remember that motivation comes from action. Taking positive action breeds *more* positive action.

Just as alcohol was the fuel for the negative feedback loop, exercise can be the fuel for the positive feedback loop. It can also be a powerful tool to help you develop in sobriety and feel good about yourself.

Nutrition And The Power Of Your Gut

As mentioned above, exercise is just one part of the equation. Let's look at how nutrition can help keep you sober.

Getting your nutrition in balance does all of these things:

- It helps you to have better sleep. Amongst a whole host of benefits, more sleep helps with insulin sensitivity (linked to cravings) and helps regulate your emotions better. You only need to have one bad night's sleep to understand how terrible you feel the next day and what type of mood it puts you in.

- It stabilises your blood sugar levels, evening out your moods and reducing cravings.
- It nourishes your liver, helping to detoxify your body (this is the polar opposite of what alcohol does!).
- It supports effective neurotransmitter function, which plays a vital role in relaying chemical signals that help control our mood, sleep cycle, digestion, and heart rate.
- It fixes deficiencies in micro and macro-nutrients. For example, if we lack sufficient iron, we could suffer from anaemia, which causes fatigue. When we feel weaker, our defences tend to drop, and we become more susceptible to making bad decisions, e.g. caving in and having a drink.
- It supports your gut health so that you can absorb essential nutrients from food. Without efficiently absorbing the nutrients our body needs, we can be left with deficiencies and disease, which can impact

mood and lead to pressing that big red button again.

I've mentioned gut health and the gut-brain axis a few times already. Here's why it's so crucial:

When people talk about a "gut feeling", it's more than just an expression. The gut is – scientifically speaking – our second brain.[47] You could even argue that it's our primary brain. This is because more nerves go from the gut to the brain than the other way around.

Nature is sending a clear message here: Take notice of your gut!

When I was drinking heavily, my gut health was horrendous. I lived with irritable bowel syndrome (IBS) and acid reflux for many years – until I finally started understanding gut health. Becoming self-aware of the problem led me to change my diet. As a result, I no longer had to live in fear around making it to the nearest toilet in time!

Your gut – along with the rest of your body – is teeming with bacteria and fungi. That sounds pretty gross, but most of it plays a crucial part in keeping you alive and healthy. There are actually more of those cells on and in your body than there are human cells.[48]

Getting your gut health on point can do all of the following things:

- Help you avoid gut dysbiosis, an imbalance of gut bacteria that can cause - among other things - weight gain, fatigue, skin conditions, anxiety, depression, and concentration issues.[49]
- Improve your heart health by encouraging "good" HDL cholesterol and triglycerides.[50] Which is vital for trying to avoid heart attacks and strokes.
- Lower your blood sugar and your risk of diabetes.[51]
- Reduce inflammation in your body. Inflammation can cause numerous diseases, including inflammatory bowel

disease, rheumatoid arthritis and psoriasis. It's also "a fundamental contributor to diseases such as cancer, diabetes and cardiovascular disease".[52]

- Ease leaky gut, IBS, acid reflux and prevent disease-causing bacteria from sticking to the intestinal walls. (Bifidobacteria and Lactobacilli, which are found in probiotics and yoghurt, are thought to help with this).[53]

Over the past decade, more and more research has emerged showing just how strong the relationship is between the gut and the brain.

"The gut-brain axis (GBA) consists of bidirectional communication between the central and the enteric nervous system, linking emotional and cognitive centres of the brain with peripheral intestinal functions. Recent advances in research have described the importance of gut microbiota in influencing these interactions."[54]

In plain English, this means how we treat our gut has a HUGE impact on how we feel. How we feel directly impacts the actions that we take. Strong gut health helps with strong sobriety. Without strong gut health, you risk low mood, anxiety, and stress. All of those things increase the chance of a relapse.

Intuition isn't just a brain thing – it's a gut thing too.

The vagus nerve connects the brain and the gut. A combination of exercise and good nutrition helps improve your vagal tone, which brings all the benefits we've discussed.

We've talked a lot about intuition. Intuition is a *gut* feeling. It interacts with subconscious thought. Making sure that the gut is well nourished – with the right foods and a good balance of bacteria - is key to making lifestyle changes that stick. And a gut that's having to process alcohol is NOT a well-nourished gut!

Where To Start With Nutrition And Your Gut Biome

Nutrition can be incredibly complicated and specific to your own circumstances. If you have the financial resources, you may wish to consider working with a registered nutritionist. It's a great way to become more self-aware and at the same time, have some accountability while you work towards the goal of improving your nutrition.

But it's not essential. You can read books about nutrition, take courses, or become more curious and self-aware about what you put into your body. As a result, you'll soon begin to "connect the dots" and start to make better food choices.

Here's a great way to start: Ask yourself how you feel after each meal. Do you feel energised and comfortably full, or do you feel lethargic and lazy? Quickly, you will see for yourself which foods energise you and which foods hold you back.

In order to build a healthy gut, it's crucial to understand how to make the *good* bacteria grow. With that in mind, let's look at pre and probiotics.

Prebiotics are specialised plant fibres that allow bacteria to grow. Think of them like the compost you need to use to grow a thriving plant – it's about setting a healthy foundation. Fruit, vegetables, oats, wholegrains and cereals are all great sources of prebiotics.

Probiotics are the live bacteria and yeasts that grow in our guts. There are lots of supplements and probiotic yoghurts that contain this "good bacteria" and claim to contribute to overall gut health.

Other more natural sources of probiotics include kefir, sauerkraut, kimchi, miso and kombucha. I have tried most of these and enjoyed them all. However, fermentation of some of these products can leave an extremely low level of alcohol as part of the process. Please check the packaging depending on your stance around alcohol in food and health drinks. The packaging should tell you the level of alcohol present, if any.

Along with exercise, cultivating good bacteria in our stomachs improves our overall vagal tone. This has an enormous impact on our mood, stress and anxiety levels. Keeping the balance is key if we want to negate feelings of low mood.

Failing to feed the gut with a healthy balance of nutritious foods that allow good bacteria to thrive and grow can seriously compromise your ability to build intuition. If you continually eat foods that put you in a low mood – such as sugary foods with little or no nutritional value - then you ARE more susceptible to relapse.

I'm not talking about a bar of chocolate each night - but if you choose to ignore what you put into your body, then you might be setting yourself on a dangerous path.

People with great intuition don't tend to live on a diet of takeaway food, sweets and chocolate!

And that brings us neatly back to sugar.

The Problem With Sugar And Relapse

Sugar and alcohol addiction are inherently linked.

A pint of cider can contain as many as five teaspoons of sugar[55] – almost as much as the daily recommended limit for adults.[56] So it's not difficult to see that when we give up our favourite drink, we might suffer from sugar withdrawal as much as alcohol withdrawal.

I used to drink 10 pints of cider on a night out. That's 250 grams of sugar – over eight times the recommended daily limit. And that doesn't even consider any sugar I had in other drinks and foods throughout that period.

The types of sugar we need to think about are "free sugars". These are:

- Any sugars added to food or drinks. These include sugars in biscuits, chocolate, flavoured yoghurts, breakfast cereals and fizzy drinks. These sugars may be added at home or by a chef or food manufacturer.

- Sugars in honey, syrups (such as maple and golden), nectars (such as blossom), and "unsweetened" fruit juices, vegetable juices and smoothies. The sugars in these foods occur naturally but still count as free sugars.

Too much sugar can lead to hypoglycaemia. Described as a "metabolic rollercoaster[57]", hypoglycaemia is the very definition of a negative feedback loop for the mind and body.

Consuming sugar (or alcohol) produces a brief high. The body then produces insulin, which is followed by low blood sugar, low mood, and a lack of energy. Next, the body produces adrenaline, and along come cravings and anxiety, generally kicked into the long grass by consuming more sugar (or alcohol).

Over time, the body becomes adrenaline fatigued. It becomes less able to produce adrenaline and more resistant to insulin. As a result, blood pressure goes up and down like a yo-yo, the metabolism slows down, and you are caught in an endless cycle of cravings.

A hypoglycaemic alcoholic doesn't only need alcohol to make their brain chemistry feel "normal". They're also having an endless battle with their blood sugar levels. It makes cravings extreme and all-consuming.

Sugar intake matters – especially when you're giving up drinking. You run the risk of confusing sugar cravings for alcohol cravings.

Of course, you can enjoy a cake, a soft drink, or an ice cream. But it will serve you well to learn to fight off cravings for sugar.

How To Fight Off Sugar Cravings

Here are some tips to help you avoid sugar cravings when you put down the bottle:

- Out of sight, out of mind. So if you know something's not good for you, don't have a stock of it in the kitchen cupboard.
- Plan ahead and work out what you're going to eat for each meal. This will stop you from grabbing something unhealthy when you're hungry.
- Eat more protein – it will help you to feel full.
- Consistently eat a breakfast that's high in fibre but low in sugar (such as wholegrain cereal or porridge). A word of warning: most cereals and cereal bars might appear healthy, but most of those I have looked at are very high in sugar. This can potentially set you up for a snacking cycle throughout the day - so check out the labels before you buy them.
- Aim for eight hours of sleep every night. Adjust your routine to make it work.
- Focus on reducing your stress levels. Stress releases more cortisol into your system, which leads to cravings. We've already

mentioned meditation, yoga, exercise and a whole host of other activities that can help reduce stress.

- Get into the habit of reading food labels. This will make you more self-aware about what you eat. **Self-aware** (what is this label telling me?) > **Positive Action** (eat healthier) > **Intuition** (you know how you feel after eating that particular food).
- Use distraction methods to keep your mouth busy. For example, chew sugar-free gum, drink herbal tea, or just use a toothpick!
- If you do enjoy sweet food, choose natural over processed – think fruit and dark chocolate rather than sweets and biscuits.
- Work on becoming an intuitive eater. Think about how everything you eat makes you feel. Is it helping or hindering you?
- Get comfortable with feeling uncomfortable. Sit with the uncomfortable craving for sugar, keep resisting, and notice how you feel. The craving *will* pass!

Another great exercise is to write a sugar diary for a week. Every time you want something sugary, write what it was, the time you craved it and the context. For example, was it straight after dinner when you wanted something sweet, or just before your favourite show on TV? Why did you reach for the snack? Were you feeling irritated?

This will help build your self-awareness around eating sugar habitually and give you the time and space to make a different choice (because it has become *conscious* to you, instead of a subconscious reaction).

You then take positive action (finding an alternative to sugar). As you reap the benefits of removing or reducing sugar, this will build healthier intuition over time. It's all around that reward link – the same mechanism as with alcohol.

The three-step process can be used for anything you want to improve, whether it's giving up alcohol, sugar, or anything else.

Much like quitting alcohol, it's good to focus not on what you're "giving up" but on what you're getting back.

You don't have to go "cold turkey" with sugar. But it's good to be mindful of how you can tackle sugar cravings while you're giving up booze. Free sugars have almost no nutritional benefit. All you're giving up is putting on weight (with its associated health issues) and constantly feeling "up and down".

***

Movement and good nutrition are powerful tools to help keep us sober and build resilience. They also have the desirable side effect of helping prevent life-threatening diseases.

Eating well and staying fit all play into the positive feedback loop that keeps on delivering and building your intuition.

There's much truth in the saying that the quality of your life depends on the quality of your thoughts. But the quality of your thoughts is also determined by how you nourish your body - through movement and what you eat.

The gut-brain axis confirms this.

When you eat well and move more, you become more **self-aware** about how it makes you feel healthier and happier. There's no denying that. Those positive feelings promote positive thoughts - which promote more **positive actions**.

The result of this positive feedback loop is that you become more in tune with an indisputable fact: How your mind feels is directly connected to how you treat your body. The more you subconsciously internalise that, the more you build your **intuition**.

Next time you exercise, take the time to be aware of how you feel before you start and how you feel 30 minutes later. Has your mood changed? Are your energy levels different?

Then, next time you eat something laden with fat and sugar, such as a pizza, Chinese takeaway or a stack of cinema munchies, do the same thing. How do you feel afterwards? How do you feel the next day? Do you feel ashamed or guilty about your choices?

The more you do this, the more you will begin to practice intuitive eating, raising your awareness of how food and exercise impact your mood, physiology, and energy.

Keeping energy in mind, we head to the final chapter. First, we've talked about the energy we put into our bodies and expel through exercise. Next, we look to understand how vibrational energy feeds into sobriety.

CHAPTER 8:

HUNGOVER ENERGY VS SOBER ENERGY: PROTECT YOUR ENERGY AT ALL COSTS

Vibrational energy might sound like a topic you'd expect to read about in the "new age therapy" section of the bookshop. But there's growing evidence that the field of vibrational medicine (or energy medicine) has a lot to offer anybody seeking to improve their health and wellbeing. Understanding the concept of energy flow is critical if you want to stay sober for the long term.

What Is Vibrational Energy?

Humans are made up of energy-producing particles that are in constant motion. So, like everyone else in the world, we are vibrating and creating energy. We even create our own energy field. Probably not something you would learn about if you spent most weekends hungover!

The concepts of vibrations and energy flow have also formed a crucial part of all kinds of practices that have been popular with millions of people for thousands of years. So are all the people who practice Chinese medicine, yoga, chakras, Qigong, feng shui, reiki, sound healing and acupuncture deluding themselves? It hardly seems likely.

Rhythms and vibrations are everywhere. In the wind, the tides, and even individual molecules that vibrate at different speeds as the weather changes. There are also numerous rhythms and vibrations in the human body – the beating of the heart, circadian rhythms, and patterns of breathing.

Many rhythms and vibrations can be measured – heart rate and blood pressure are two examples. But it may surprise you to know that scientists have managed to detect vibrations in areas "smaller than 1/1000th the diameter of a single human hair".[58]

Those who advocate for the awareness of vibrational energy believe that "it's possible to speed up or slow down the vibrations that occur at the cellular and atomic levels by changing our thoughts, behaviours — and even our surroundings".

If you doubt the value of embracing the importance of vibrational energy, consider the following things:

- How your heart races and your body reacts if you think you've left your wallet or bag on the train that's just left the station.
- How spending time with certain people consistently leaves you tired and drained.
- How listening to the right song at the right time can transform your mood. (Sound and music are all created from vibrations.)
- How you can sometimes walk into a room and immediately detect a negative vibe or bad blood between people present.

It seems pretty clear that we're built to detect and absorb the energy around us.

The theory of vibrational energy assumes that some people, places, feelings and things can have low vibrational energy and others have high vibrational energy. For example, negative emotions such as anger and fear are thought to vibrate at a lower rate than feelings of peace and joy.

Why Vibrational Energy Is Important And How To Manage It

The aim is to design your life around absorbing lots of good (high) energy and avoiding bad (low) energy. Once again, self-awareness is key. The more you become aware of how different people, places, feelings and things impact your energy, the more you can take the right actions to create the life you want.

Think about what being hungover feels like. That's some negative, low-vibing energy right there.

Regular drinkers tend to be "low-vibers". They may be nice people, but they have their own reasons for their habit – perhaps unresolved trauma of their own, or general unhappiness with their lives. (It's worth noting, at this point, that alcohol doesn't transform somebody into a "high-viber" – it just makes them drunk!)

By contrast, consider a group of sober people at the end of an exercise class, a park run or a hobby group. They'll seem happy and glow with energy. They *are* "high-vibers" - well nourished, well exercised, and absorbing positive energy from people with a shared interest.

This might all sound "new age" to you. Trust me, it took a bit of time to overcome my own initial reservations. But the fact is that people (including you) give off good energy or bad. What you do in your day-to-day life will positively charge those vibrations or negatively charge them. You have ultimate control in how that plays out.

Sobriety allows you to start truly understanding yourself and your energy levels. You can work out which people, places, feelings and things give you a boost and which bring you down.

Positive emotions and thoughts bring you high-vibing energy. Being around other sober people who are working on becoming better versions of themselves feels vastly different to sitting in a pub. Often, those places are full of people being snarky about others and moaning about their lot in life. (I was one of them).

If you want to fuel your positive feedback loops, it's essential to spend your time with high-vibing people – in high-vibing places, doing high-vibing things. Most of the ideas we've explored in this book contribute to that too - positive thoughts, emotions, and a healthy body all help contribute to being positively charged.

Here are several ways to positively increase your vibrational frequency:

- Hang around positive people on a similar path of self-discovery and personal growth. As motivational speaker Jim Rohn said, "we are the average of the five people we spend the most time with."[59]
- Spend time in positive places: the gym, the theatre, the cinema, the bowling alley, the library, and the homes of family and friends who make you feel good about yourself. Don't spend all your time in places that continually make you question your sobriety, such as bars and clubs!
- Exercise! It's a Catch-22, but you do have to exercise regularly to feel energetic. We already mentioned how vital exercise is for creating more available energy in your body.
- Eat nutritious food. The energy you eat is just as vital as the energy that comes from your thoughts and emotions.
- Look to therapies that incorporate energy flow, such as reiki, sound healing and yoga. Set aside any preconceptions you may have

- and just do it. You will be surprised by how powerful these activities are for clearing blockages and building up your energy levels.

- Spend as much time as possible in nature. Scientific evidence is building up around the power of grounding and reconnecting with the earth. Studies show positive improvements in fatigue, chronic pain, anxiety, and even blood pressure.[60] The perfect excuse to play more golf, hit the beach or hug that tree you've been eyeing up!
- Take sober holidays. They give you a chance to *truly* rejuvenate and are a world away from holidays where you put your mind and body through even more abuse than you do at home!
- Work on being truly present and "in the moment" in everything you do. It's a great way to channel energy positively. You're sure to have had plenty of conversations with people who nod their head when you

know they're not really listening. Don't be one of those people.

- Avoid "energy thieves". There are almost certainly people out there who leave you tired and drained after every interaction. That drained feeling is your self-awareness at work – it's telling you that those people aren't doing you much good. So spend as little time as possible with people who make you feel like that.
- Become passionate about things: Salsa dancing, kung fu, collecting records, climbing mountains – anything that makes your soul sing and gives you positive energy.

When your thoughts, emotions and actions are aligned, you will feel at your best. The more you become **self-aware** and take **positive actions** for your own energy levels, the more those things become **intuitive**.

You'll intuitively turn down invitations to events that will leave you feeling drained and negative, like saying no or having an exit strategy for after-work drinks on Thursday night. You'll intuitively know whether a decision will take you closer to your goal of staying sober or further away from it.

But over time, you will become a Jedi in energy flow and understand that where your attention goes – your energy flows. So if you want to be sober, focus all your energy on becoming sober.

You won't regret it.

Chapter 9:

Conclusion: Bringing It All Together

This book gives you lots to think about and take in. Nobody expects you to implement every strategy and remember every detail straight away. That would be overwhelming and unrealistic. Changing your life is a journey.

No doubt certain concepts and ideas will have resonated with you more than others. So grab those and run with them while focussing on that one big goal: not drinking for 24 hours at a time.

I'd encourage you to revisit these words repeatedly. You'll likely find different "eureka moments" each time you read, especially as you progress along your own unique journey to sobriety.

To bring things full circle, let's revisit the fundamental premise of the book: *3 Sober Steps* to help you to stop drinking and stay sober:

1. **Working on your self-awareness** in every possible way will help you to understand *why* you drink. This is essential if you wish to live a sober life for the long-term, rather than getting stuck in a cycle of quitting and relapsing.
2. **Taking positive action** – with dedication and consistency – will put you in the category of those who've quit drinking rather than those who talk about it (and do nothing about it).
3. **Building intuition** will happen over time as a direct result of becoming more self-aware, taking the right actions to move you towards your goals, and becoming used to experiencing the many pleasures that come from a healthy and sober life.

The *3 Sober Steps* won't always happen in sequence. Sometimes you might get an intuitive feeling that something isn't right, which will allow you to start the self-awareness journey as the second step.

As we said at the start, it's fair to argue that staying sober is harder than quitting drinking. **Self-awareness, positive action** and **intuition** are the things you need to make a lasting change – one where the rewards and the positive feedback loops keep coming.

I've *been* the drinker who passionately believed that people who weren't getting hammered every Friday night was somehow "missing out". I've *been* the drinker who was utterly convinced I'd never cope with the "boredom" of not drinking. I've *been* the drinker who came out with meaningless nonsense like "you can never trust someone who doesn't drink."

I only wish I'd discovered the reality of sobriety sooner – living an authentic, fulfilled life full of discovery, variety, and the irreplaceable feeling that the person you see in the mirror might be someone you like and respect.

Something that always stands out in sober communities is how much happiness and positive energy flies around. Getting sober is like being let in on a secret. It's not something that people regret. If it were, people would celebrate when they relapsed. They don't.

That feeling of consistent happiness and positivity is available to everyone – including you. And with the unstoppable rise of the "sober curious" movement, more and more people are experiencing it. All it takes is committing to a goal of not drinking for 24 hours at a time.

What are you waiting for?

Leave A 1-Click Review

Customer reviews

5 out of 5

16 global ratings

5 star	100%
4 star	0%
3 star	0%
2 star	0%
1 star	0%

How are ratings calculated?

Review this product

Share your thoughts with other customers

Write a customer review

I would be incredibly grateful if you could spare 60 seconds to leave a review on Amazon, even if it's just a few sentences.

HAVE YOU READ THE INTERNATIONAL BEST SELLER.......

.....Sober On A Drunk Planet:
Giving Up Alcohol......

Or Visit:

www.soberonadrunkplanet.com/books

Also Available On Amazon
(Kindle/Paperback/Hardcover/Audible)

If you want to join a community of like-minded souls.........

Scan the QR code below

Or visit

www.soberonadrunkplanet.com/community

YOUR FREE GIFT

Scan QR code below

Get your FREE 10-minute guided meditation to help build your practice of self-awareness by scanning the QR code or use the link below

bit.ly/3TdTRPr

Resources

Sober On A Drunk Planet – Podcast

https://www.soberonadrunkplanet.com/podcasts/

Follow Us On Instagram:

https://www.instagram.com/soberonadrunkplanet/

Physical Withdrawals – More Information:

Drink Aware:

https://www.drinkaware.co.uk/facts/health-effects-of-alcohol/mental-health/alcohol-withdrawal-symptoms

NHS:

https://www.nhs.uk/conditions/alcohol-misuse/treatment/

Alcohol Change:

https://alcoholchange.org.uk/

Web MD:

https://www.webmd.com/mental-health/addiction/alcohol-withdrawal-symptoms-treatments#1

Citations

[1] Mail Online. (2011, May 9). Pass the painkillers: The average Brit spends more than five YEARS of their life with a hangover. Retrieved from https://www.dailymail.co.uk/health/article-1385024/The-average-Brit-spends-5-YEARS-life-hangover.html

[2] DiLonardo, M. (2021, November 26). What Is Alcohol Withdrawal? Retrieved from https://www.webmd.com/mental-health/addiction/alcohol-withdrawal-symptoms-treatments#1

[3] Oxford Learner's Dictionaries. Self-awareness (noun). Retrieved from https://www.oxfordlearnersdictionaries.com/definition/english/self-awareness

[4] Duval, S & Wicklund, R. (1972). *A Theory of Objective Self Awareness*. Academic Press.

[5] Quote Investigator. Between Stimulus and Response There Is a Space. In That Space Is Our Power To Choose Our Response. Retrieved from https://quoteinvestigator.com/2018/02/18/response/

[6] Alcohol, Drugs and Development. (2012, October 21). Half the world's adults do not drink alcohol – what should the policy implications be? Retrieved from http://www.add-resources.org/half-the-worlds-adults-do-not-drink-alcohol-what-should-the-policy-implications-be.5325474-315773.html

[7] Mayo Clinic. Chronic stress puts your health at risk. Retrieved from https://www.mayoclinic.org/healthy-lifestyle/stress-management/in-depth/stress/art-20046037

[8] MedicalNewsToday. Cognitive dissonance: What to know. Retrieved from https://www.medicalnewstoday.com/articles/326738

[9] NHS. Drink Less. Retrieved from https://www.nhs.uk/better-health/drink-less/

[10] Tikvah Lake. (2020, November 19). How Cognitive Dissonance relates to Alcohol Abuse. Retrieved from https://www.tikvahlake.com/blog/how-cognitive-dissonance-relates-to-alcohol-abuse/

[11] Vilhaue, J. (2020, September 27). How Your Thinking Creates Your Reality. Retrieved from https://www.psychologytoday.com/us/blog/living-forward/202009/how-your-thinking-creates-your-reality

[12] Quote Investigator. Faced With the Choice Between Changing One's Mind and Proving That There Is No Need To Do So, Almost Everyone Gets Busy On the Proof. Retrieved from https://quoteinvestigator.com/2018/05/17/change-view/

[13] Jarrett, C. (2016, September 9). Clues to your personality appeared before you could talk. Retrieved from https://www.bbc.com/future/article/20160907-clues-to-your-personality-appeared-before-you-could-talk

[14] Bajalan, D. (2020, March 9). Using history to understand the present. https://news.missouristate.edu/2020/03/09/using-history-to-understand-the-present/

[15] Kaliszewski, M. (2022, September 9). The Link Between Child Abuse and Substance Abuse. Retrieved from https://americanaddictioncenters.org/blog/the-link-between-child-abuse-and-substance-abuse

[16] Tony Robbins. Reprogram your Mind. Retrieved from https://www.tonyrobbins.com/mind-meaning/how-to-reprogram-your-mind/

[17] Quote Investigator. Do One Thing Every Day That Scares You. Retrieved from https://quoteinvestigator.com/2013/08/09/scare/

[18] Cherry, K. (2022, February 18). What Is Neuroplasticity? Retrieved from https://www.verywellmind.com/what-is-brain-plasticity-2794886

---

[19] Taylor, A. (2020, January 27). The Right to Listen. Retrieved from https://www.newyorker.com/news/the-future-of-democracy/the-right-to-listen

[20] Kerpen, D. 15 Quotes to Inspire You to Be a Better Listener. Retrieved from https://www.inc.com/dave-kerpen/15-quotes-to-inspire-you-to-become-a-better-listener.html

[21] Nhat Hanh, T. (2010). *Reconciliation: Healing the Inner Child.* Parallax Press.

[22] Kane, R. (2022, September 6). How Many People Meditate In The World? Retrieved from https://mindfulnessbox.com/how-many-people-meditate-in-the-world/

[23] Schultz, J. (2020, July 24). 5 Differences Between Mindfulness and Meditation. Retrieved from https://positivepsychology.com/differences-between-mindfulness-meditation/

[24] Solaris Pediatric Therapy. The Importance of the Vagal Nerve and the Nervous System. Retrieved from https://www.solarispediatrictherapy.com/blog/the-importance-of-the-vagal-nerve-and-the-nervous-system

[25] Solanki, D & Lane, A. (2010). Relationships between Exercise as a Mood Regulation Strategy and Trait Emotional Intelligence. 1(4): 195–200. Retrieved from https://www.ncbi.nlm.nih.gov/pmc/articles/PMC3289183/

[26] Daily Stoic. Marcus Aurelius Quotes. Retrieved from https://dailystoic.com/marcus-aurelius-quotes/

[27] UWA Online. (2019, May 17). Our Basic Emotions. Retrieved from https://online.uwa.edu/infographics/basic-emotions/

[28] He's Extraordinary. Improve Emotional Regulation In Just 7 Minutes Per Day. Retrieved from https://hes-extraordinary.com/improve-emotional-regulation-just-7-minutes-per-day

[29] Rees Anderson, A. (2015, April 7). Resentment Is Like Taking Poison And Waiting For The Other Person To Die. Retrieved from https://www.forbes.com/sites/amyanderson/2015/04/07/resentment-is-like-taking-poison-and-waiting-for-the-other-person-to-die/?sh=186a1172446c

[30] Keller, A. (2020, February 28). Alcohol and Dopamine. Retrieved from https://www.drugrehab.com/addiction/alcohol/alcoholism/alcohol-and-dopamine/

[31] Stewart, J. (2008). Psychological and neural mechanisms of relapse. 363(1507): 3147–3158. Retrieved from https://www.ncbi.nlm.nih.gov/pmc/articles/PMC2607321/

[32] Jedras, P, Jones A & Field M. (2013). The role of anticipation in drug addiction and reward. 2014(3): 1 -10. Retrieved from https://www.dovepress.com/the-role-of-anticipation-in-drug-addiction-and-reward-peer-reviewed-fulltext-article-NAN

[33] Pratt, M. (2022, February 17). The Science of Gratitude. Retrieved from https://www.mindful.org/the-science-of-gratitude/

[34] Emmons, R. A, & McCullough, M. E. (2003). Counting Blessings Versus Burdens: An Experimental Investigation of Gratitude and Subjective Well-Being in Daily Life. 84(2), 377. Retrieved from https://greatergood.berkeley.edu/pdfs/GratitudePDFs/6Emmons-BlessingsBurdens.pdf

[35] AlcoholThinkAgain. Alcohol and the Digestive System. Retrieved from https://alcoholthinkagain.com.au/alcohol-your-health/alcohol-and-long-term-health/alcohol-and-the-digestive-system/

[36] Recovery Nutrition. How Nutrition Can Support Becoming Alcohol-Free. Retrieved from https://www.recovery-nutrition.co.uk/blog/nutrition-to-support-being-alcohol-free

[37] Wellness Retreat. Sugar and Dopamine: The Link Between Sweets and Addiction. Retrieved from

---

https://wellnessretreatrecovery.com/sugar-and-dopamine-link-sweets-addiction/

[38] WebMD. (2021, April 12). What to Know About VO2 Max. Retrieved from https://www.webmd.com/fitness-exercise/what-to-know-about-vo2-max

[39] Bird, S. & Hawley, J. (2017). Update on the effects of physical activity on insulin sensitivity in humans. 2(1): e000143. Retrieved from https://www.ncbi.nlm.nih.gov/pmc/articles/PMC5569266/

[40] Hep. (2016, December 19). Diet and Exercise Improve Liver and Kidney Health in Those With NASH. Retrieved from https://www.hepmag.com/article/diet-exercise-improve-liver-kidney-health-nash

[41] WebMD. (2022, February 10). Diet and Lifestyle Tips to Reverse Fatty Liver Disease. Retrieved from https://www.webmd.com/hepatitis/fatty-liver-disease-diet

[42] Healthline. (2019, January 30). How Aerobic Classes Can Make You a Better Problem Solver. Retrieved from https://www.healthline.com/health-news/want-to-be-a-better-problem-solver-try-doing-aerobics

[43] Pacheco, D. (2022, May 6). Exercise and Sleep. Retrieved from https://www.sleepfoundation.org/physical-activity/exercise-and-sleep

[44] Pacheco, D. (2022, September 19). Alcohol and Sleep. Retrieved from https://www.sleepfoundation.org/nutrition/alcohol-and-sleep

[45] NHS. Benefits of Exercise. Retrieved from https://www.nhs.uk/live-well/exercise/exercise-health-benefits/

[46] Singh, D. (2022, June 20). How yoga can help us heal from past trauma. Retrieved from https://www.indiatoday.in/news-analysis/story/how-yoga-can-help-us-heal-from-past-trauma-1964598-2022-06-20

[47] Gerrie, H. Our second brain: More than a gut feeling. Retrieved from https://neuroscience.ubc.ca/our-second-brain-more-than-a-gut-feeling/

[48] Looi, M. (2020, July 14). The human microbiome: Everything you need to know about the 39 trillion microbes that call our bodies home. Retrieved from https://www.sciencefocus.com/the-human-body/human-microbiome/

[49] WebMD. (2021, June 9). What Is Dysbiosis? Retrieved from https://www.webmd.com/digestive-disorders/what-is-dysbiosis

[50] Fu, J, Bonder, M, Cenit, M, Tigchelaar, E, Maatman, A, Dekens, J, Brandsma, E, Marczynska, J, Imhann, F, Weersma, R, Franke, L, Poon, T, Xavier, R, Gevers, D, Hofker, M, Wijmenga, C, & Zhernakova, A. (2015). The Gut Microbiome Contributes to a Substantial Proportion of the Variation in Blood Lipids. 117(9):817-24. Retrieved from https://pubmed.ncbi.nlm.nih.gov/26358192/

[51] Nutritious Life. How Gut Health Impacts Blood Sugar. Retrieved from https://nutritiouslife.com/eat-empowered/gut-health/gut-health-blood-sugar/

[52] Lucas, S, Rothwell, N, & Gibson, R. (2006). The role of inflammation in CNS injury and disease. 147(Suppl 1): S232–S240. Retrieved from https://www.ncbi.nlm.nih.gov/pmc/articles/PMC1760754/

[53] Healthline. Why the Gut Microbiome Is Crucial for Your Health. Retrieved from https://www.healthline.com/nutrition/gut-microbiome-and-health

[54] Carabotti, M, Scirocco, A, Maselli, M, & Severi, C. (2015). The gut-brain axis: interactions between enteric microbiota, central and enteric nervous systems. 28(2): 203–209. Retrieved from https://www.ncbi.nlm.nih.gov/pmc/articles/PMC4367209/

[55] Greatist. The Hard Choice: Is Beer or Cider Better? Retrieved from https://greatist.com/health/beer-or-cider-healthier

---

[56] NHS. Sugar: the facts. Retrieved from https://www.nhs.uk/live-well/eat-well/food-types/how-does-sugar-in-our-diet-affect-our-health

[57] FitRecovery. The Links Between Hypoglycaemia and Alcohol and How to Fix It. Retrieved from https://fitrecovery.com/alcoholism-and-hypoglycemia/

[58] Healthline. What Is Vibrational Energy? Retrieved from https://www.healthline.com/health/vibrational-energy

[59] Groth, A. (2012, July 14). You're The Average Of The Five People You Spend The Most Time With. Retrieved from https://www.businessinsider.com/jim-rohn-youre-the-average-of-the-five-people-you-spend-the-most-time-with-2012-7?r=US&IR=T

[60] Healthline. Grounding: Exploring Earthing Science and the Benefits Behind It. Retrieved from https://www.healthline.com/health/grounding

CPSIA information can be obtained
at www.ICGtesting.com
Printed in the USA
LVHW051040230423
744862LV00001B/122